Healthy Eating for Two
Second edition

By Don Orwell

http://SuperfoodsToday.com

Copyright © 2015 by Don Orwell.

All legal rights reserved. You cannot offer this book for free or sell it. You do not have reselling legal rights to this book. This eBook may not be recreated in any file format or physical format without having the expressed written approval of Don Orwell. All Violators will be sued.

While efforts have been made to assess that the information contained in this book is valid, neither the author nor the publisher assumes any accountability for errors, interpretations, omissions or usage of the subject matters herein.

Disclaimer:

The Information presented in this book is created to provide useful information on the subject areas discussed. The publisher and author are not accountable for any particular health or allergic reaction needs that may involve medical supervision and are not liable for any damage or damaging outcomes from any treatment, application or preparation, action, to any person reading or adhering to the information in this book. References are presented for informational reasons only and do not represent an endorsement of any web sites or other sources. Audience should be informed that the websites mentioned in this book may change.

This publication includes opinions and ideas of its author and is meant for informational purposes only. The author and publisher shall in no event be held liable for any damage or loss sustained from the usage of this publication.

Your Free Gift

As a way of saying thanks for your purchase, I'm offering you my FREE eBook that is exclusive to my book and blog readers.

Superfoods Cookbook - Book Two has over 70 Superfoods recipes and complements Superfoods Cookbook Book One and it contains Superfoods Salads, Superfoods Smoothies and Superfoods Deserts with ultra-healthy non-refined ingredients. All ingredients are 100% Superfoods.

It also contains Superfoods Reference book which is organized by Superfoods (more than 60 of them, with the list of their benefits), Superfoods spices, all vitamins, minerals and antioxidants. Superfoods Reference Book lists Superfoods that can help with 12 diseases and 9 types of cancer.

http://www.SuperfoodsToday.com/FREE

Table of Contents

Healthy Eating for Two 1

    Superfoods Introduction 14

Cookbook for Two 18

Condiments 18

    Basil Pesto 18

    Cilantro Pesto 19

    Sundried Tomato Pesto 21

Broths 22

    Vegetable broth 22

    Chicken Broth 24

    Beef Broth 25

Pastes 27

    Curry Paste 27

    Tomato paste 29

    Precooked beans 31

Breakfast - Oatmeal 32

    Superfoods Oatmeal Breakfast 32

    Oatmeal Yogurt Breakfast 34

    Cocoa Oatmeal 35

    Flax and Blueberry Vanilla Overnight Oats 37

    Apple Oatmeal 38

    Almond Butter Banana Oats 39

    Coconut Pomegranate Oatmeal 41

    Walnut Oatmeal with Fresh Blueberries 42

- Raspberry Oatmeal 42
- Almonds, Cinnamon & Almond Milk Oatmeal 44

Savory Breakfasts 45
- Omelet with Leeks 45
- Egg pizza crust 46
- Omelet with Superfoods veggies 47
- Egg Muffins 49
- Smoked Salmon Scrambled Eggs 50
- Steak and Eggs 52
- Egg Bake 54
- Frittata 56
- Superfoods Naan / Pancakes / Crepes 58
- Zucchini Pancakes 59
- Savory Superfoods Pie Crust 61
- Quiche 63
- Frittata with Broccoli and Tomato 65
- Frittata with Green and Red Peppers 66

Superfoods Smoothies 67
- Fruits and Veggies preparation 69

GREEN SMOOTHIES 70
- Kale Kiwi Smoothie 70
- Zucchini Apples Smoothie 71
- Dandelion Smoothie 72
- Fennel Honeydew Smoothie 73

Broccoli Apple Smoothie 74

Salad Smoothie 75

Avocado Kale Smoothie 76

Watercress Smoothie 77

Beet Greens Smoothie 78

Broccoli Leeks Cucumber smoothie 79

Cacao Spinach Smoothie 80

Flax Almond Butter Smoothie 81

Apple Kale Smoothie 82

Iceberg Peach Smoothie 83

Rainbow Smoothie 84

3 Colors Rainbow Smoothie 84

Salad Dressings 85

Italian Dressing 85

Yogurt Dressing 85

Salads 86

Large Fiber Loaded Salad with Italian Dressing 86

Large Fiber Loaded Salad with Yogurt Dressing 87

Large Fiber Loaded Salad as a meal on its own 88

Greek Salad 90

Strawberry Spinach Salad 92

Tuna Bean Salad 94

Cucumber, Cilantro, Quinoa Tabbouleh 95

Almond, Quinoa, Red Peppers & Arugula Salad 96

- Asparagus, Quinoa & Red Peppers Salad 97
- Chickpeas, Quinoa, Cucumber & Tomato Salad 99
- Quinoa Salad.. 100
- Cauliflower & Eggs Salad 102
- Quinoa & Almond Superfoods Tabbouleh 103
- Greek Cucumber Salad 105
- Mediterranean Salad 107
- Pomegranate Avocado salad 109
- Roasted Beet Salad 110
- Apple Coleslaw 111
- Chickpeas, Quinoa, Radish & Cucumber Salad................................. 113
- Steak, Broccoli & Mushrooms Salad... 114
- Arugula, Quinoa, Red Peppers & Almonds Salad 115
- Pumpkin, Quinoa, Cheese & Arugula Salad.. 116
- Pear, Quinoa, Spinach & Grapes Salad 117
- Asparagus, Quinoa & Carrot Salad 118
- Pork, Red Quinoa, Carrot & Pumpkin Salad 119
- Chicken, Roasted Veggies & Arugula Salad 120
- Broccoli, Quinoa, Shrimps & Scallops Salad 121
- Shrimp, Figs, Lettuce & Orange Salad 122

Appetizers... 122
- Hummus 123
- Guacamole... 125
- Baba Ghanoush.. 126

- Espinacase la Catalana 128
- Tapenade 129
- Red Pepper Dip 130
- *Roasted Garlic* 132
- Eggplant and Yogurt 133
- Caponata 134

Soups 136
- Cream of Broccoli Soup 136
- Lentil Soup 138
- Cold Cucumber Avocado Soup 140
- Bouillabaisse 141
- Gaspacho 143
- Italian Beef Soup 144
- Creamy roasted mushroom 146
- Black Bean Soup 148
- Ajoblanco con uvas 150
- Squash soup 152
- Kale White Bean Pork Soup 154
- Avgolemono – Greek lemon chicken soup 156
- Egg-Drop Soup 158
- Creamy Tomato Basil Soup 160
- Minestrone 161

Grilled Meats & Salad 163
- Chicken and Large Fiber Loaded Salad with Italian Dressing 163

- Salmon with Large Fiber Loaded Salad with Italian Dressing 164
- Ground Beef Patty with Large Fiber Loaded Salad with Yogurt Dressing 165
- Lean Pork with Fiber Loaded Salad with Yogurt Dressing 166
- Caribbean Chicken salad 167
- Herb Crusted Salmon 169
- Tuna with Large Fiber Loaded Salad with Italian Dressing 170

Stews, Chilies and Curries 172

- Stuffed Peppers with beans 172
- Vegetarian Chili 174
- Lentil Stew 176
- Braised Green Peas with Beef 177
- White Chicken Chili 179
- Kale Pork 181
- 30-Minute Squash Cauliflower and Green Peppers Coconut Curry . 183
- Crockpot Red Curry Lamb 185
- Easy Lentil Dhal 186
- Gumbo 188
- Chickpea Curry 191
- Red Curry Chicken 192
- Braised Green Beans with Pork 193
- Ratatouille 195
- Barbecued Beef 197
- Beef Tenderloin with Roasted Shallots 199
- Chili 201

Glazed Meatloaf	203
Eggplant Lasagna	205
Stuffed Eggplant	207
Stuffed Red Peppers with Beef	208
Superfoods Goulash	210
Frijoles Charros	211
Chicken Cacciatore	213
Cabbage Stewed with Meat	215
Beef Stew with Peas and Carrots	217
Green Chicken Stew	219
Irish Stew	221
Hungarian Pea Stew	223
Chicken Tikka Masala	225
Greek Beef Stew (Stifado)	227
Meat Stew with Red Beans	229
Lamb and Sweet Potato Stew	231
Beef, Parsnip, Celery Stew	232
Chicken Mushrooms & Olives Stew	234
Chicken Pasanda Curry	236
Osso Bucco & Garlic Stew	238
Beef Meatballs with White Beans	240
Duck Stew	242
Pork, Zucchini, Pork, Tomato & Corn Stew	244
Red Peppers Pork Curry	245

- Beef Ratatouille 246
- Chicken, Green Peas and Red Peppers Stew 247
- Crock Pot Turkey Roast Mediterranean style 248
- Slow Cooker Pot Roast 249
- Black Bean, Chicken & Brown Rice Stew 250
- Duck Curry 251
- Eggplant Red Pepper Stew 252
- Irish Lamb Stew 253
- Shrimp, Onion & Cilantro Stew 254
- Venison Green Beans Onion Stew 255
- Pork Cauliflower Stew 256
- Sweet Potato Veal Stew 257
- Pork Broccoli Carrot Stew 257
- Moroccan Lamb & Mushrooms Stew 259
- Shrimp Peppers Stew 260

Brown Rice Dishes 261
- Paella 261
- Asparagus Mint Lemon Risotto 263

Stir Fries 265
- Pork and Bok Choy / Celery Stir Fry 265
- Lemon Chicken Stir Fry 266
- Pan seared Brussels sprouts 268
- Beef and Broccoli Stir Fry 269
- Garbanzo Stir Fry 270

- Thai Basil Chicken 272
- Shrimp with Snow Peas 274
- Pork and Green Beans Stir Fry 276
- Cashew chicken 277
- Meats 279
  - Baked Chicken Breast with Fresh Basil 279
  - Roast Chicken with Rosemary 280
  - Carne Asada 281
- Meatballs 282
  - Baked Beef Meatballs 282
  - Middle Eastern Meatballs 284
- Casseroles 286
  - Broccoli Chicken Casserole 286
  - Beef Meatballs Broccoli Casserole 288
  - Beef Meatballs Cauliflower Casserole 290
  - Cabbage Roll Casserole 292
  - Pork Chop Casserole 294
  - Mushrooms Casserole 295
  - Chicken Eggplant Casserole 297
  - Beef Meatballs Green Beans Casserole 299
- "Breaded" "fried" food 301
  - Breaded Tilapia 301
  - Breaded Chicken 303
  - Lemon Pork with Asparagus 305

- Pizza 307
  - Meat Pizza 307
- Side dishes 309
  - Green Superfoods Rice 309
  - Roasted curried cauliflower 311
  - Roasted cauliflower with Tahini sauce 313
  - Baked Sweet Potatoes 314
  - Asparagus with mushrooms and hazelnuts 315
  - *Chard and Cashew Sauté* 317
  - Cauliflower rice side dish 318
- Crockpot 319
  - Slow Cooker Pepper Steak 319
  - Pork Tenderloin with peppers and onions 321
  - Beef Bourguinon 323
  - Italian Chicken 324
  - Slow Cook Jambalaya 326
  - Ropa Vieja 328
  - Lemon Roast Chicken 330
  - Fall Lamb and Vegetable Stew 332
  - Slow cooker pork loin 334
  - Sauerbraten 336
- Fish 338
  - Cioppino 338
  - Flounder with Orange Coconut Oil 340

- Grilled Salmon 341
- Crab Cakes 343

Sweets 345
- Superfoods Dark Chocolate 345
- Fruits dipped in Superfoods chocolate 346
- Superfoods No-Bake Cookies 348
- Raw Brownies 350
- Superfoods No Bake Balls / Cookies 351
- Superfoods Ice cream 352
- Apple Spice Cookies 353
- Superfoods Macaroons 354
- Superfoods Stuffed Apples 355
- Whipped Coconut cream 356
- Granola Mix 358
- "Peanut" Butter Truffles 360
- Pumpkin Brownies 362
- Vegan Sesame Seeds Cookies 364
- Coconut Cream Tart 366
- Raw Vegan Reese's Cups 368
- Raw Vegan Coffee Cashew Cream Cake 369

Superfoods Reference Book 372
Other Books from this Author 374

Superfoods Introduction

Superfoods are high in fiber, thermogenic, low in saturated fat, have tons of antioxidants, probiotic, vitamins, minerals, high in Omega 3 fats and above all tasty.

Superfoods Diet works because it's return to the type of food your body naturally craves and was designed for. Whole foods Superfoods is the food humans consumed for literally millions of years. Superfoods are nutritionally dense foods that are widely available and which offer tremendous dietary and healing potential. Superfoods Diet is the only diet that doesn't restrict any major type of food. If features:

• Healthy Fats: Olive Oil, Nuts, Seeds, Coconut Oil, Avocado

• Proteins: Salmon, Beans, Organic Chicken, Grass-Fed Beef, Pork Tenderloin, Lentils

• Non-gluten Carbs: Fruits, Vegetables, Oats, Brown Rice, Quinoa, Buckwheat

• Simple non-processed Dairy: Greek Yogurt, Farmer's Cheese, Goat Cheese

• Antioxidants: Garlic, Ginger, Turmeric, Cacao, Cinnamon, Berries

What Superfoods are NOT:

- **Not** processed or refined foods
- **Not** preservatives, additives or artificial coloring
- **Not** smoked food or processed meats
- **Not** canned vegetables or meats (beans, garbanzos, beets, corned beef) except canned fish (sardines, tuna) once or twice a week
- **Not** wheat, refined flour, or sugar.
- **Not** corn, white rice, or potatoes. Brown rice and quinoa are fine.
- **Not** vegetable oils or fried food. Olive oil and Coconut oil are fine.
- **Not** soy products or tofu
- **Not** pasta, except gluten-free soba noodles (100% buckwheat) or acorn or mung bean noodles.
- **Not** full-fat dairy cheese. Yogurt, kefir and low-fat farmers' cheese/cottage cheese/Greek feta cheese are fine and occasionally (context-related) some low-fat cheddar or mozzarella are fine. "Context-related" means it's okay to sprinkle some grated low-fat cheddar or mozzarella on your casseroles or a Superfoods pizza.
- **Not** store-bought salad dressings or condiments with vegetable oils or corn syrup (mayo, ketchup, barbeque sauce). Hummus, guacamole, mustard, pesto and hot sauces are fine.

Superfoods meals have existed for ages, and you will find some Superfoods recipes in Mediterranean, Chinese, Japanese and European cookbooks. Superfoods cuisine is mainly comprised of soups, salads, stews and grilled meats and veggies. Some examples of well-known Superfoods recipes are hummus, guacamole, tapenade, basic chicken or beef soup with vegetables and without noodles, any slow cooked stew with leaner meats and veggies, some bean dishes without ketchup and sugar, some lentil dishes and curries, salads without store-bought dressing, pasta, bacon or bread, any grilled lean fish or meat and veggie. A lot of other classical recipes can be easily modified and become

Superfoods stars. For example, you can swap white rice for brown rice and omit sugar and soy in Japanese recipes. You can also swap rice, sauce thickener, soy and oil in Chinese stir-fries with healthier options.

I don't believe in any diet that restricts any type of food in the long term, except diets that exclude processed industrial foods. We have witnessed what the industrial food did to modern society and that is not the option to go with! Yo-Yo Nation should switch to Superfoods and not junk food!

Let me mention the last reason why I'm sure that the Superfoods Diet will change your life forever. Once you know everything about the benefits of the vast array of Superfoods, and once you learn why processed food is so bad on so many levels, I'm pretty sure that you will think twice every time you get served any processed food and I'm sure that you will keep thinking, "Why am I eating this, why am I ruining my health? I can do better, there is tasty food that will help me with my inflammations and that will protect me from cancer."

Once you expand your knowledge, you can't go back and forget about all the facts about Superfoods and all the facts about processed food. And if you have kids, I'm pretty sure that you will think twice before you serve them processed colored foods instead of healthy, tasty Superfoods meals.

Some people either hate to cook or they don't have enough time to do so, but it's obvious that Superfoods Diet will require some time to shop for fresh foods and some time for preparing them. The good news is that 90% of the meals are very easy and quick to prepare. Let me give you some examples of Superfoods meals that require only 10 minutes prep time:

- You can chop veggies while you grill meat or fish.

- Stir-fries are typically prepared in 10 minutes.

- Slow cooker meals or casseroles or stews are also typically prepared in 10 minutes or less. In all of them you typically include chopped onions, carrots, meat and one more veggie (green peas, green beans, mushrooms, eggplants, red peppers etc.). And you just pour all ingredients in a pot, casserole or slow cooker and you're done.

Monitoring the stew as it cooks is not a huge time-wasting task (same with monitoring a casserole in the oven). You can prepare a large pot or casserole once a week, freeze some of it, and eat it once or twice during the week. If you prepare 2 such meals on a Sunday, you're set for the week.

• Superfoods breakfasts are very quick; eggs or oatmeal don't take too much time to make.

My point is that you can eat healthy if you are mentally prepared to shop for healthy ingredients as well as a healthy meal preparation. If you have a bunch of kids and 2 jobs, you can still find 2-3 hours on a Sunday evening to prepare all these foods for the rest of the week. Buy already-cut bags of spinach and cabbage and other veggies and only add olive oil, lemon or apple cider vinegar and salt before you eat them. Cut some veggies for salads and snacks on a Sunday evening, put it in your Tupperware container, and you're set for 2-3 days. At the same time, cook a stew in the huge pot and load food in the slow cooker. Then freeze all that cooked food so that you'll have meals on hand for when you don't have time to do preparations. Keep a bunch of hard-boiled eggs in your fridge for snacks. Be over-prepared for your weight loss journey. You're about to become a Superfoodie!! Read the Superfoodie Manifesto.

• Spike any salad dressing with 1 Tbsp. of Spirulina, Chlorella, Maca or Matcha . Chlorella has a strong taste (think pond water or horse hay ☺), Spirulina has oceanic taste (think seaweed or something fishy), Maca has earthy/nutty taste (goes well with smoothies) and Matcha is basically a powdered green tea, so you know the taste. Spirulina and seaweeds taste best in some veggie soup or any fish stew. It tastes nasty in average smoothies, but some strong taste can hide it (think grapefruit, lemon, lime, pomegranate or granny Smith apples).

All recipes are for two, except some desserts which might have some leftovers.

Cookbook for Two

Allergy labels: SF – Soy Free, GF – Gluten Free, DF – Dairy Free, EF – Egg Free, V - Vegan, NF – Nut Free

Condiments

Basil Pesto
- 1 cup basil
- 1/3 cup cashews
- 2 garlic cloves, chopped
- 1/2 cup <u>olive</u> oil or <u>avocado</u> oil

Process basil, cashews and garlic until smooth. Add oil in a slow stream. Process to combine. Transfer to a bowl. Season with salt and pepper. Stir to combine. Allergies: SF, GF, DF, EF, V

Cilantro Pesto

- 1 cup cilantro
- 1/3 cup cashews
- 2 garlic cloves, chopped
- 1/2 cup olive oil or avocado oil

Process cilantro, cashews and garlic. Add oil in a slow stream. Process to combine. Transfer to a bowl. Season with salt and pepper. Stir to combine. Allergies: SF, GF, DF, EF, V

Sundried Tomato Pesto

- 3/4 cup sundried tomatoes
- 1/3 cup cashews
- 2 garlic cloves, chopped
- 1/2 cup olive oil or cumin oil

Process tomato, cashews and garlic. Add oil in a slow stream. Process to combine. Transfer to a bowl. Season with salt and pepper. Stir to combine. Allergies: SF, GF, DF, EF, V

Broths

Some recipes require a cup or more of various broths, vegetable, beef or chicken broth. I usually cook the whole pot and freeze it.

Vegetable broth

Servings: 6 cups

Ingredients

- 1 tbsp. coconut oil
- 1 large onion
- 2 stalks celery, including some leaves
- 2 large carrots
- 1 bunch green onions, chopped
- 8 cloves garlic, minced
- 8 sprigs fresh parsley
- 6 sprigs fresh thyme
- 2 bay leaves
- 1 tsp. salt
- 2 quarts water

Instructions - Allergies: SF, GF, DF, EF, V, NF

Chop veggies into small chunks. Heat oil in a soup pot and add onion, scallions, celery, carrots, garlic, parsley, thyme, and bay leaves. Cook over high heat for 5 to 7 minutes, stirring occasionally.

Bring to a boil and add salt. Lower heat and simmer, uncovered, for 30 minutes. Strain. Other ingredients to consider: broccoli stalk, celery root

Chicken Broth

Ingredients

- 4 lbs. fresh chicken (wings, necks, backs, legs, bones)
- 2 peeled onions or 1 cup chopped leeks
- 2 celery stalks
- 1 carrot
- 8 black peppercorns
- 2 sprigs fresh thyme
- 2 sprigs fresh parsley
- 1 tsp. salt

Instructions - Allergies: SF, GF, DF, EF, NF

Put cold water in a stock pot and add chicken. Bring just to a boil. Skim any foam from the surface. Add other ingredients, return just to a boil, and reduce heat to a slow simmer. Simmer for 2 hours. Let cool to warm room temperature and strain. Keep chilled and use or freeze broth within a few days. Before using, defrost and boil.

Beef Broth

Ingredients

- 4-5 pounds beef bones and few veal bones
- 1 pound of stew meat (chuck or flank steak) cut into 2-inch chunks
- Olive oil
- 1-2 medium onions, peeled and quartered
- 1-2 large carrots, cut into 1-2 inch segments
- 1 celery rib, cut into 1 inch segments
- 2-3 cloves of garlic, unpeeled
- Handful of parsley, stems and leaves
- 1-2 bay leaves
- 10 peppercorns

Instructions - Allergies: SF, GF, DF, EF, NF

Heat oven to 375°F. Rub olive oil over the stew meat pieces, carrots, and onions. Place stew meat or beef scraps, stock bones, carrots and onions in a large roasting pan. Roast in oven for about 45 minutes, turning everything half-way through the cooking.

Place everything from the oven in a large stock pot. Pour some boiling water in the oven pan and scrape up all of the browned bits and pour all in the stock pot.

Add parsley, celery, garlic, bay leaves, and peppercorns to the pot. Fill the pot with cold water, to 1 inch over the top of the bones. Bring the stock pot to a regular simmer and then reduce the heat to low, so it just barely simmers. Cover the pot loosely and let simmer low and slow for 3-4 hours.

Scoop away the fat and any scum that rises to the surface once in a while.

After cooking, remove the bones and vegetables from the pot. Strain the broth. Let cool to room temperature and then put in the refrigerator.

The fat will solidify once the broth has chilled. Discard the fat (or reuse it) and pour the broth into a jar and freeze it.

Pastes

Curry Paste

This should not be prepared in advance, but there are several curry recipes that are using curry paste and I decided to take the curry paste recipe out and have it separately. So, when you see that the recipe is using curry paste, please go to this part of the book and prepare it from scratch. Don't use processed curry pastes or curry powder; make it every time from scratch. Keep the spices in original form (seeds, pods), ground them just before making the curry paste. You can dry heat in the skillet cloves, cardamom, cumin and coriander and then crush them coarsely with mortar and pestle.

Ingredients

- 2 onions, minced
- 2 cloves garlic, minced
- 2 teaspoons fresh ginger root, finely chopped
- 6 whole cloves
- 2 cardamom pods
- 2 (2 inch) pieces cinnamon sticks, crushed
- 1 tsp. ground cumin
- 1 tsp. ground coriander
- 1 tsp. salt
- 1 tsp. ground cayenne pepper
- 1 tsp. ground turmeric

Instructions - Allergies: SF, GF, DF, EF, V, NF

Heat oil in a frying pan over medium heat and fry onions until transparent. Stir in garlic, cumin, ginger, cloves, cinnamon, coriander, salt, cayenne, and turmeric. Cook for 1 minute over medium heat, stirring constantly. At this point other curry ingredients should be added.

HEALTHY EATING FOR TWO

Tomato paste

Some recipes (chili) require tomato paste. I usually prepare 20 or so liters at once (when tomato is in season, which is usually September) and freeze it.

Ingredients

- 5 lbs. chopped plum tomatoes
- 1/4 cup extra-virgin olive oil or avocado oil plus 2 tbsp.
- salt, to taste

Instructions - Allergies: SF, GF, DF, EF, V, NF

Heat 1/4 cup of the oil in a skillet over medium heat. Add tomatoes. Season with salt. Bring to a boil. Cook, stirring, until very soft, about 8 minutes.

Pass the tomatoes through the finest plate of a food mill. Push as much of the pulp through the sieve as possible and leave the seeds behind.

Bring it to boil, lower it and then boil uncovered, so the liquid will thicken (approx. 30-40 minutes). That will give you homemade tomato juice. You get tomato paste if you boil for 60 minutes, it gets thick like store bought ketchup.

Store sealed in an airtight container in the refrigerator for up to one month, or freeze, for up to 6 months.

Precooked beans

Again, some recipes require that you cook some beans (butter beans, red kidney, garbanzo) in advance. Cooking beans takes around 3 hours and it can be done in advance or every few weeks and the rest get frozen. Soak beans for 24 hours before cooking them. After the first boil, throw the water, add new water and continue cooking. Some beans or lentils can be sprouted for few days before cooking and that helps people with stomach problems.

Breakfast - Oatmeal

Superfoods Oatmeal Breakfast
Allergies: SF, GF, DF, EF, V, NF

- 1 1/2 cup oatmeal
- 2 tsp. of ground flax seeds
- 2 tsp. of sunflower seeds
- A dash of cinnamon
- 1 tsp. of cocoa

Cook oatmeal with hot water and after that mix all ingredients. Sweeten if you have to with few drops of raw honey. Optional: You can replace sunflower seeds with pumpkin seed or chia seed. You can add a handful of blueberries or any berries instead of cocoa.

Oatmeal Yogurt Breakfast

Allergies: SF, GF, EF, NF

- 1 cup dry oatmeal
- Handful of blueberries (optional)
- 2 cups of low-fat yogurt

Mix all ingredients and wait 20 minutes or leave overnight in the fridge if using steel cut oats.

Cocoa Oatmeal

Ingredients - Allergies: SF, GF, DF, NF

- 1 cup dry oats
- 3 cups water
- A pinch tsp. salt
- 1 tsp. ground vanilla bean
- 3 tbsp. cocoa powder
- 2 tbsp. raw honey
- 3 tbsp. ground flax seeds meal
- a dash of cinnamon
- 3 egg whites

Instructions

In a saucepan over high heat, place the oats and salt. Cover with 3 cups water. Bring to a boil and cook for 3-5 minutes, stirring occasionally. Keep adding 1/2 cup water if necessary as the mixture thickens.

In a separate bowl, whisk 4 tbsp. water into the 3 tbsp. cocoa powder to form a smooth sauce. Add the vanilla to the pan and stir.

Turn the heat down to low. Add the egg whites and whisk immediately. Add the flax meal, and cinnamon. Stir to combine. Remove from heat, add raw honey and serve immediately.

Topping suggestions: sliced strawberries, blueberries or few almonds.

Flax and Blueberry Vanilla Overnight Oats

Ingredients - Allergies: SF, GF, EF, V, NF

- 1 cup oats
- 2/3 cup water
- 1/2 cup low-fat yogurt
- 1 tsp. ground vanilla bean
- 2 tbsp. flax seeds meal
- A pinch of salt
- Blueberries, almonds, blackberries, raw honey for topping

Instructions

Add the ingredients (except for toppings) to the bowl in the evening. Refrigerate overnight.

In the morning, stir up the mixture. It should be thick. Add the toppings of your choice.

Apple Oatmeal

Ingredients - Allergies: SF, GF, DF, EF, V, NF

- 2 grated apple
- 1 cup oats
- 2 cups water
- Dash of cinnamon
- 4 tsp. raw honey

Instructions

Cook the oats with the water for 3-5 minutes.

Add grated apple and cinnamon. Stir in the raw honey.

Almond Butter Banana Oats

Ingredients - Allergies: SF, GF

- 1 cup oats
- 1 1/2 cups water
- 2 egg white
- 2 bananas
- 2 tbs. flax seeds meal
- 2 tsp raw honey
- pinch cinnamon
- 1 tbs. almond butter

Instructions

Combine oats and water in a bowl. Beat the egg white, then whisk it in with the uncooked oats. Boil on stovetop. Check consistency and continue to heat as necessary until the oats are fluffy and thick. Mash banana and add to oats. Heat for 1 minute

Stir in flax, raw honey, and cinnamon. Top with almond butter!

Coconut Pomegranate Oatmeal

Ingredients - Allergies: SF, GF, DF, EF, V, NF

- 1 cup oats
- 2/3 cup coconut milk
- 2 cups water
- 4 tbs. shredded unsweetened coconut
- 2 tbs. flax seeds meal
- 2 tbs. raw honey
- 6 tbs. pomegranate seeds

Instructions

Cook oats with the coconut milk, water, and salt.

Stir in the coconut, raw honey and flaxseed meal. Sprinkle with extra coconut and pomegranate seeds.

Walnut Oatmeal with Fresh Blueberries

Serves 1

Ingredients - Allergies: SF, GF, DF, EF, V

- 1 cup blueberries
- 1 cup oats
- 2 cups water
- 3/4 cup walnuts
- Dash of cinnamon
- 4 tsp. raw honey

Instructions

Cook the oats with the water for 3-5 minutes.

Add walnuts and cinnamon. Stir in the raw honey. Top with blueberries

Raspberry Oatmeal

Serves 1

Ingredients - Allergies: SF, GF, DF, EF, V

- 1 cup raspberries
- 1 cup oats
- 2 cup water
- 3/4 cup sesame seeds
- Dash of cinnamon
- 2 tsp. raw honey

Instructions

Cook the oats with the water for 3-5 minutes.

Add sesame seeds and cinnamon. Stir in the raw honey. Top with raspberries

Almonds, Cinnamon & Almond Milk Oatmeal

Serves 1

Ingredients - Allergies: SF, GF, EF, V, NF

- 1 cup oats
- 1 1/2 cup water
- 1/2 cup low-fat almond milk
- 1 tsp. cinnamon
- 4 tbsp. whole almonds

Instructions

Cook the oats with the water for 3-5 minutes. Mix in vanilla and honey. Top with blueberries and sunflower seeds.

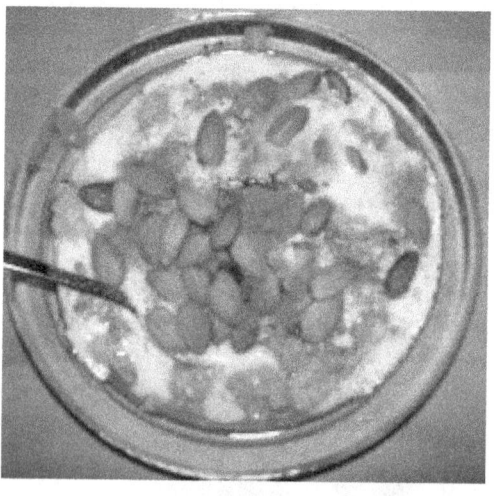

Savory Breakfasts

Omelet with Leeks
Allergies: SF, GF, DF, NF

Cook 1 cup chopped leeks in little coconut oil until they get soft and then mix the 4 beaten eggs in.

Egg pizza crust

Ingredients - Allergies: SF, GF, DF, NF
- 4 eggs
- 1/2 cup of coconut flour
- 1 cup of coconut milk
- 1 crushed garlic clove

Mix and make an omelet.

Omelet with Superfoods veggies

Ingredients - Allergies: SF, GF, DF, NF

- 4 large eggs
- Salt
- Ground black pepper
- 2 tsp. olive oil or cumin oil
- 2 cups spinach, cherry tomatoes and 1 spoon of yogurt cheese
- Crushed red pepper flakes and a pinch of dill (optional)

Instructions

Whisk 4 large eggs in a bowl. Season with salt and ground black pepper and set aside. Heat 1 tsp. olive oil in a medium skillet over medium heat. Add baby spinach, tomatoes, cheese and cook, tossing, until wilted (Approx. 1 minute). Add eggs; cook, stirring occasionally, until just set, about 1 minute. Stir in cheese. Sprinkle with crushed red pepper flakes and dill.

Egg Muffins

Ingredients - Allergies: SF, GF, DF, NF

Serving: 4 muffins

- 4 eggs
- 1/2 cup diced green bell pepper
- 1/2 cup diced onion
- 1/2 cup spinach
- 1/4 tsp. salt
- 1/8 tsp. ground black pepper
- 2 tbsp. water

Instructions

Heat the oven to 350 degrees F. Oil 4 muffin cups. Beat eggs together. Mix in bell pepper, spinach, onion, salt, black pepper, and water. Pour the mixture into muffin cups. Bake in the oven until muffins are done in the middle.

Smoked Salmon Scrambled Eggs

Ingredients, serves 2 - Allergies: SF, GF, DF, NF

- 1 tsp <u>coconut oil</u>
- 4 eggs
- 1 Tbs water
- 4 oz smoked salmon, sliced
- 1/2 avocado
- ground black pepper, to taste
- 4 chives, minced (or use 1 green onion, thinly sliced)

Instructions

Heat a skillet over medium heat. Add coconut oil to pan when hot. Meanwhile, scramble eggs. Add eggs to the hot skillet, along with smoked salmon. Stirring continuously, cook eggs until soft and fluffy. Remove from heat. Top with avocado, black pepper, and chives to serve.

HEALTHY EATING FOR TWO

Steak and Eggs

Serves 2

Ingredients - Allergies: SF, GF, DF, NF

- 1/2 lb boneless beef steak or pork tenderloin
- 1/4 tsp ground black pepper
- 1/4 tsp sea salt (optional)
- 2 tsp coconut oil
- 1/4 onion, diced
- 1 red bell pepper, diced
- 1 handful spinach or arugula
- 2 eggs

Instructions

Season sliced steak or pork tenderloin with sea salt and black pepper. Heat a sauté pan over high heat. Add 1 tsp coconut oil, onions, and meat when pan is hot, and sauté until steak is slightly cooked. Add spinach and red bell pepper, and cook until steak is done to your liking. Meanwhile, heat a small fry pan over medium heat. Add remaining coconut oil, and fry two eggs. Top each steak with a fried egg to serve.

Egg Bake

Ingredients - Allergies: SF, GF, DF, NF

- 1 cup chopped red peppers or spinach
- 1/2 cup zucchini
- 1 tbsp. coconut oil
- 1/2 cup sliced mushrooms
- 1/4 cup sliced green onions
- 4 eggs
- 1/2 cup coconut milk
- 1/4 cup almond flour
- 1 tbsp. minced fresh parsley
- 1/4 tsp. dried basil
- 1/4 tsp. salt
- 1/8 tsp. ground black pepper

Instructions

Preheat oven to 350 degrees F. Put coconut oil in a skillet. Heat it to medium heat. Add mushrooms, onions, zucchini and red pepper (or spinach) until vegetables are tender, about 5 minutes. Drain veggies and spread them over the baking dish.

Beat eggs in a bowl with milk, flour, parsley, basil, salt, and pepper. Pour egg mixture into baking dish.

Bake in preheated oven until the center is set (approx. 35 to 40 minutes).

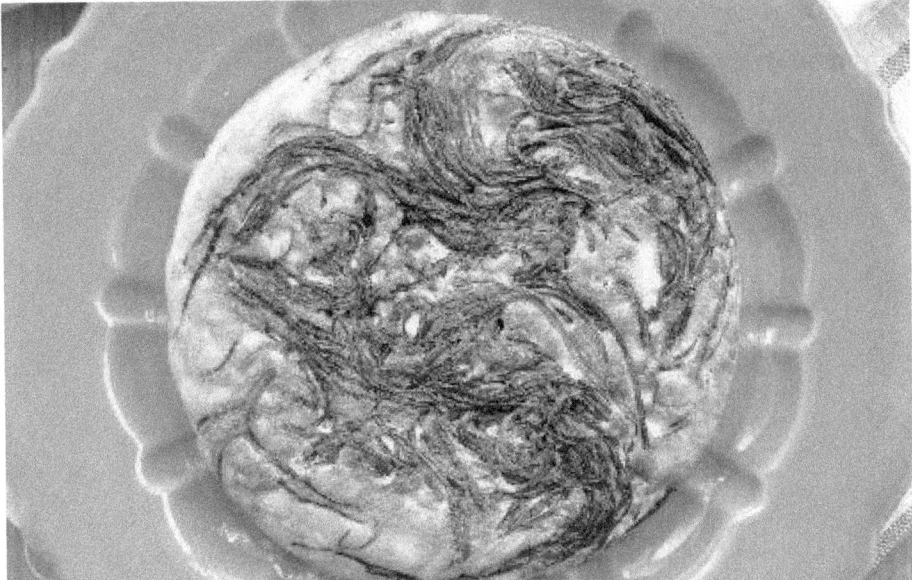

Frittata

Ingredients - Allergies: SF, GF, DF, NF

- 2 tbsp. olive oil or avocado oil
- 1 small Zucchini, sliced
- 1/2 cup torn fresh spinach
- 1 tbsp. sliced green onions
- 1/2 tsp. crushed garlic, salt and pepper to taste
- 1/4 cup coconut milk
- 4 eggs

Instructions

Heat olive oil in a skillet over medium heat. Add zucchini and cook until tender. Mix in spinach, green onions, and garlic. Season with salt and pepper. Continue cooking until spinach is wilted.

In a separate bowl, beat together eggs and coconut milk. Pour into the skillet over the vegetables. Reduce heat to low, cover, and cook until eggs are firm (5 to 7 minutes).

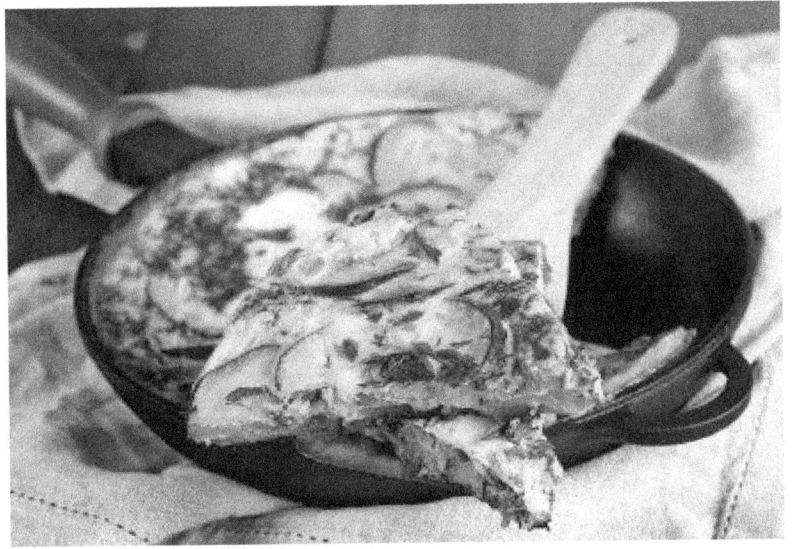

Superfoods Naan / Pancakes / Crepes

Ingredients - Allergies: SF, GF, DF, EF, V

- 1/2 cup almond flour
- 1/2 cup Tapioca Flour
- 1 cup Coconut Milk
- Salt
- coconut oil

Instructions

Mix all the ingredients together.

Heat a pan over medium heat and pour batter to desired thickness. Once the batter looks firm, flip it over to cook the other side.

If you want this to be a dessert crepe or pancake, then omit the salt. You can add minced garlic or ginger in the batter if you want, or some spices.

Zucchini Pancakes

Ingredients - Allergies: SF, GF, DF

- 1 medium zucchini
- 2 tbsp. chopped onion
- 3 beaten eggs
- 6 tbsp. almond flour
- 1 tsp. salt
- 1/2 tsp. ground black pepper
- coconut oil

Instructions

Heat the oven to 300 degrees F.

Grate the zucchini into a bowl and stir in the onion and eggs. Stir in 6 tbsp. of the flour, salt, and pepper.

Heat a large sauté pan over medium heat and add coconut oil in the pan. When the oil is hot, lower the heat to medium-low and add batter into the pan. Cook the pancakes about 2 minutes on each side, until browned. Place the pancakes in the oven.

Savory Superfoods Pie Crust

Ingredients - Allergies: SF, GF, DF

- 1 cups blanched almond flour
- 1/4 cup tapioca flour
- 1/2 tsp. finely ground sea salt
- 1/2 tsp. paprika
- 1/4 tsp. ground cumin
- 1/8 tsp. ground white pepper
- 2 Tbsp. coconut oil
- 1 large egg

Instructions

Instructions

Place almond flour, tapioca flour, sea salt, vanilla, egg and coconut sugar (if you use coconut sugar) in the bowl of a food processor. Process 2-3 times to combine. Add oil and raw honey (if you use raw honey) and pulse with several one-second pulses and then let the food processor run until the mixture comes together. Move dough onto a plastic wrap sheet. Wrap and then press the dough into a 9-inch disk. Refrigerate for 30 minutes.

Remove plastic wrap. Press dough onto the bottom and up the sides of a 7-inch buttered pie dish. Crimp a little bit the edges of crust. Cool in the refrigerator for 20 minutes. Put the oven rack to middle position and preheat oven to 375F. Put in the oven and bake until golden brown.

Quiche

Ingredients - Allergies: SF, GF, DF, NF

- 1 Precooked and cooled Savory Superfoods Pie Crust
- 6 ounces organic spinach, cooked and drained
- 4 ounces cubed pork
- 1 medium shallots, thinly sliced and sautéed
- 3 eggs
- 1/2 cup coconut milk
- 1/2 tsp. salt
- 1/8 tsp. freshly ground black pepper

Instructions

Brown the pork in coconut oil and then add the spinach and shallots. Set aside once done.

Preheat oven to 350F. In a large bowl, combine eggs, milk, salt and pepper. Whisk until foamy. Add in about 3/4 of the drained filling mixture, reserving the other 1/4 to "top" the quiche. Pour egg mixture into crust and place remaining filling on top of the quiche.

Place quiche in oven in the center of the middle rack and bake undisturbed for 45 to 50 minutes.

Frittata with Broccoli and Tomato

Serves 2

Ingredients - Allergies: SF, GF, DF, NF

- 4 eggs
- Salt
- Ground black pepper
- 2 tsp. olive oil or cumin oil
- 1 cup broccoli & 1 cup sliced tomatoes
- Crushed red pepper flakes and a 2 Tbsp. chopped chives (optional)

Instructions

Whisk eggs in a small bowl. Season with salt and ground black pepper and set aside. Heat oil in a medium skillet over medium heat. Add broccoli and tomatoes and cook, tossing, approx. 1 minute. Add eggs; cook, stirring occasionally, until just set, about 1 minute. Sprinkle with crushed red pepper flakes and chives.

Frittata with Green and Red Peppers
Serves 2

Ingredients - Allergies: SF, GF, DF, NF

- 4 eggs
- Salt
- Ground black pepper
- 2 tsp. olive oil or avocado oil
- 1 cup each chopped green and red peppers

Instructions

Whisk eggs in a small bowl. Season with salt and ground black pepper and set aside. Heat olive oil in a medium skillet over medium heat. Add peppers and cook, tossing approx. 1 minute. Add eggs; cook, stirring occasionally, until just set, about 1 minute.

Superfoods Smoothies

Put the liquid in first. Surrounded by tea or yogurt, the blender blades can move freely. Next, add chunks of fruits or vegetables. Leafy greens are going into the pitcher last. Preferred liquid is green tea, but you can use almond or coconut milk or herbal tea.

Start slow. If your blender has speeds, start it on low to break up big pieces of fruit. Continue blending until you get a puree. If your blender can pulse, pulse a few times before switching to a puree mode. Once you have your liquid and fruit pureed, start adding greens, very slowly. Wait until previous batch of greens has been completely blended. I use blenders because they're sturdy and offer 7 year warranty. That was definitely the best investment in my health.

Thicken? Added too much tea or coconut milk? Thicken your smoothie by adding ice cubes, flax meal, chia seeds or oatmeal. Once you get used to various tastes of smoothies, add any seaweed, spirulina, chlorella powder or ginger for additional kick. Experiment with any Superfoods in powder form at this point. Think of adding any nut butter or sesame paste too or some Superfoods oils.

Rotate! Rotate your greens; don't always drink the same smoothie! At the beginning try 2 different greens every week and later introduce third and fourth one weekly. And keep rotating them. Don't use spinach and kale all the time. Try beets greens, they have a pinch of pink in them and that add great color to your smoothie. Here is the list of leafy green for you to try: spinach, kale, dandelion, chards, beet leaves, arugula, lettuce, collard greens, bok choy, cabbage, cilantro, parsley.

Flavor! Flavor smoothies with ground vanilla bean, cinnamon, ½ tsp. of lucuma powder, nutmeg, cloves, almond butter, cayenne pepper, ginger or just about any seeds or chopped nuts combination.

Not only are green smoothies high in nutrients, vitamins and fiber, they can also make any vegetable you probably don't like (be it kale, spinach or broccoli) taste great. The secret behind blending the perfect smoothie is using sweet fruits or nuts or seeds to give your drink a unique taste.

There's a reason kale and spinach seem to be the main ingredients in almost every green smoothie. Not only do they give smoothies their verdant color, they are also packed with calcium, protein and iron.

Although blending alone increases the accessibility of carotenoids, since the presence of fats is known to increase carotenoid absorption from leafy greens, it is possible that coconut oil, nuts and seeds in a smoothie could increase absorption further.

Fruits and Veggies preparation

- Wash fruits and veggies
- Pluck leaves and stems from berries
- Core apples (optional)
- Peel orange, lemon, lime, grapefruit, kiwi, beet, pomegranate, ginger, dragon fruit and banana
- Peel and take the seeds out of papaya
- Remove seeds from peppers, apricots, peaches, cherries, plums and prunes
- Mangos, melons and avocados should be peeled, and inner seed taken out
- Watermelons should have their outer rind removed.
- Scoop out the flesh from passion fruit
- Cut fruits and veggies in 2-inch slices

If you can't find some ingredient, replace it with the closest one.

All details about each ingredient (vitamins, minerals, antioxidants etc.) can be found in my free Superfoods Reference book: http://www.SuperfoodsToday.com/FREE

GREEN SMOOTHIES

Kale Kiwi Smoothie
- 1 cup Kale, chopped
- 2 Apples
- 3 Kiwis
- 1 tablespoon flax seeds
- 1 tablespoon royal jelly
- 1 cup crushed ice

Zucchini Apples Smoothie

- 1/2 cup zucchini
- 2 Apples
- 3/4 avocado
- 1 stalk Celery
- 1 Lemon
- 1 tbsp. Spirulina
- 1 1/2 cups crushed ice

Dandelion Smoothie

- 1 cup Dandelion greens
- 1 cup Spinach
- ½ cup tahini
- 1 Red Radish
- 1 tbsp. chia seeds
- 1 cup lavender tea

Fennel Honeydew Smoothie

- ½ cup fennel

- 1 cup Broccoli

- 1 tbsp. Cilantro

- 1 cup Honeydew

- 1 cup crushed ice

- 1 tbsp. Chlorella

Broccoli Apple Smoothie

- 1 Apple
- 1 cup Broccoli
- 1 tbsp. Cilantro
- 1 Celery stalk
- 1 cup crushed ice
- 1 tbsp. crushed Seaweed

Salad Smoothie

- 1 cup spinach
- ½ cucumber
- 1/2 small onion
- 2 tablespoons Parsley
- 2 tablespoons lemon juice
- 1 cup crushed ice
- 1 tbsp. olive oil or cumin oil
- ¼ cup Wheatgrass

Avocado Kale Smoothie

- 1 cup Kale
- ½ Avocado
- 1 cup Cucumber
- 1 Celery Stalk
- 1 tbsp. chia seeds
- 1 cup chamomile tea
- 1 tbsp. Spirulina

Watercress Smoothie

- 1 cup Watercress
- ½ cup almond butter
- 2 small cucumbers
- 1 cup coconut milk
- 1 tbsp. Chlorella
- 1 tbsp. Black cumin seeds – sprinkle on top and garnish with parsley

Beet Greens Smoothie

- 1 cup Beet Greens
- 2 tbsp. Pumpkin seeds butter
- 1 cup Strawberry
- 1 tbsp. Sesame seeds
- 1 tbsp. hemp seeds
- 1 cup chamomile tea

Broccoli Leeks Cucumber smoothie

- 1 cup Broccoli
- 2 tbsp. Cashew butter
- 2 Leeks
- 2 Cucumbers
- 1 Lime
- ½ cup Lettuce
- ½ cup Leaf Lettuce
- 1 tbsp. Matcha
- 1 cup crushed ice

Cacao Spinach Smoothie

- 2 cups spinach
- 1 cup blueberries, frozen
- 1 tablespoons dark cocoa powder
- ½ cup unsweetened almond milk
- 1/2 cup crushed ice
- 1 tsp raw <u>honey</u>
- 1 tbsp. Matcha powder

Flax Almond Butter Smoothie

- ½ cup plain yogurt
- 2 tablespoons almond butter
- 2 cups spinach
- 1 banana, frozen
- 3 strawberries
- 1/2 cup crushed ice
- 1 teaspoon flax seeds

Apple Kale Smoothie

- 1 cup kale
- ½ cup coconut milk
- 1 tbsp. Maca
- 1 banana, frozen
- ¼ teaspoon cinnamon
- 1 Apple
- Pinch of nutmeg
- 1 clove
- 3 ice cubes

Iceberg Peach Smoothie

- 1 cup Iceberg lettuce
- 1 Banana
- 1 peach
- 1 Brazil Nut
- 1 Mango
- 1 cup Kombucha
- Top with <u>hemp</u> seeds

Rainbow Smoothie

3 Colors Rainbow Smoothie

- Blend 1 Large beet with some crushed ice

- Blend 3 carrots with some crashed ice

- Blend 1 cucumber, 1 cup of leaf lettuce and ½ cup Wheatgrass

- Serve them separate to preserve the distinct color

Salad Dressings

Italian Dressing

Allergies: SF, GF, DF, EF, V, NF

- 2 tsp. olive oil or avocado oil
- lemon
- minced garlic
- salt

Yogurt Dressing

Allergies: SF, GF, DF, EF, V, NF

- 1 cup of plain low-fat Greek yogurt or low-fat buttermilk
- 1 tsp. olive oil or avocado oil
- minced garlic
- salt
- lemon

Occasionally I would add a tsp. of mustard or some herbs like basil, oregano, marjoram, chives, thyme, parsley, dill or mint. If you like spicy hot food, add some cayenne in the dressing. It will speed up your metabolism and have interesting hot spicy effect in cold yogurt or buttermilk.

Salads

Large Fiber Loaded Salad with Italian Dressing

Allergies: SF, GF, EF, NF

- 2 cups of spinach
- 1 cup of shredded cabbage, sauerkraut or lettuce. Cabbage has more substance.
- Italian or Yogurt dressing
- Cayenne pepper (optional)
- Few sprigs of cilantro (optional)
- 2 spring (green) onions (optional)

Large Fiber Loaded Salad with Yogurt Dressing

Serves 1 - Allergies: SF, GF, EF, NF

- 2 cups of spinach
- 1 cup of shredded cabbage or lettuce. Cabbage has more substance.
- Italian or Yogurt dressing
- Cayenne pepper (optional)
- Few sprigs of cilantro (optional)
- 2 spring (green) onions (optional)

Large Fiber Loaded Salad as a meal on its own

Allergies: SF, GF, EF, NF

This is what I eat every second evening and I can't get enough of it!!! This is the real secret to lose weight while having full stomach with grade A ingredients!!

- 2 cup of spinach
- 2 cup of shredded cabbage
- Yogurt dressing
- Cayenne pepper (optional)
- Few sprigs of cilantro (optional)
- 3 spring (green) onions
- 10 o.z. low-fat farmers' cheese

Pour yogurt dressing into the salad bowl. Add farmers' cheese and mix thoroughly. Cut spring onions in small pieces and add to the cheese mixture and mix. Add spinach and cabbage and mix thoroughly. Add spices (optional).

Greek Salad

Allergies: SF, GF, EF, NF

- 1 head romaine lettuce
- 1/2 lb. plump tomatoes
- 3 oz. Greek or black olives, sliced
- 2 oz. sliced radishes
- 4 oz. low-fat feta or goat cheese
- 2 oz. anchovies (optional)

Dressing:
- 2 oz. olive oil or avocado oil
- 2 oz. fresh lemon juice
- 1/2 tsp. dried oregano
- 1/4 tsp. black pepper
- 1/4 tsp. salt
- 2 cloves garlic, minced

Wash and cut lettuce into pieces. Slice tomatoes in quarters. Combine olives, lettuce, tomatoes, and radishes in large bowl. Mix dressing ingredients together and toss with vegetables. Pour out into a shallow serving bowl. Crumble feta/goat cheese over all, and arrange anchovy fillets on top (if desired).

Strawberry Spinach Salad

Ingredients - Allergies: SF, GF, DF, EF, V

- 1 tbsp. black sesame seeds
- 1 tbsp. poppy seeds
- 1/4 cup olive oil or cumin oil
- 1/8 cup lemon juice
- 1/8 tsp. paprika
- 1/2 bag fresh spinach - chopped, washed and dried
- 1 cup strawberries, sliced
- 1/4 cup toasted slivered almonds

Instructions

Whisk together the sesame seeds, olive oil, poppy seeds, paprika, lemon juice and onion. Refrigerate.
In a large bowl, combine the spinach, strawberries and almonds. Pour dressing over salad. Toss and refrigerate 15 minutes before serving.

Tuna Bean Salad

Allergies: SF, GF, DF, EF, NF

Ingredients

- 2 cans tuna in water, drained
- 1/2 cup four bean mix (or just white or red beans), drained, rinsed
- 1 tomato, deseeded, chopped
- 1 large celery stick, trimmed, finely chopped
- 1 small onion, halved, thinly sliced
- 1/2 cup flat-leaf parsley leaves, chopped
- 1/2 lemon, rind finely grated, juiced
- 2 garlic cloves, crushed & 1 tbsp. extra-virgin olive oil or avocado oil

Mix all ingredients and serve.

Cucumber, Cilantro, Quinoa Tabbouleh

Serves 2

Ingredients - Allergies: SF, GF, DF, EF, NF, V

- 1 cup cooked quinoa mixed with 1 tbsp. sesame seeds
- 1/2 cup chopped tomato and green pepper
- 1 cup chopped cucumber
- 1/2 cup chopped cilantro

Dressing:
- 1 tbsp. olive oil or avocado oil
- 1 tbsp. fresh lemon juice
- pinch of black pepper
- pinch of sea salt

Instructions: Mix all ingredients.

Almond, Quinoa, Red Peppers & Arugula Salad

Serves 2

Ingredients - Allergies: SF, GF, DF, EF, NF, V

- 1 cup cooked quinoa mixed with 1 tbsp. pumpkin seeds
- 1/2 cup chopped almonds
- 1 cup chopped arugula
- 1/2 cup sliced red peppers

Dressing:
- 1 tbsp. olive oil or cumin oil
- 1 tbsp. fresh lemon juice
- pinch of black pepper
- pinch of sea salt

Instructions: Mix all ingredients.

Asparagus, Quinoa & Red Peppers Salad

Serves 2

Ingredients - Allergies: SF, GF, DF, EF, NF, V

- 1 cup cooked quinoa mixed with 1 tbsp. sunflower seeds
- 1 cup sliced red peppers
- 1 cup grilled asparagus
- Garnish with lime and parsley

Dressing:
- 1 tbsp. olive oil or avocado oil
- 1 tbsp. fresh lemon juice
- pinch of black pepper
- pinch of sea salt

Instructions: Mix all ingredients.

Chickpeas, Quinoa, Cucumber & Tomato Salad

Serves 2

Ingredients - Allergies: SF, GF, DF, EF, NF, V

- 1 cup cooked quinoa mixed with 1 tbsp. sesame seeds
- 1 cup cooked chickpeas
- 1 cup chopped cucumber and green onions
- 1/2 cup chopped tomato

Dressing:
- 1 tbsp. olive oil or avocado oil
- 1 tbsp. fresh lemon juice
- pinch of black pepper
- pinch of sea salt

Instructions: Mix all ingredients.

Quinoa Salad

Ingredients - Allergies: SF, GF, EF

For the salad

- 1 cups cooked quinoa
- 1+1/2 cup frozen green peas
- 1/2 cup low-fat feta cheese
- 6 oz. pork, cubed
- 1/4 cup freshly chopped basil and cilantro
- 1/4 cup almonds, pulsed in a food processor until crushed

For the dressing

- 1/4 cup lemon juice (1-2 large juicy lemons)
- 1/4 cup olive oil or cumin oil
- 1/8 tsp. salt (more to taste)
- 1 teaspoon raw honey , to taste

Instructions

Bring a pot of water to boil and then lower the heat. Add the peas and cook covered until bright green. In the meantime, brown pork in a skillet. Toss the quinoa with the pork, peas, feta, herbs, and almonds.

Puree all the dressing ingredients in the food processor. Toss the dressing with the salad ingredients. Season generously with salt and pepper. Serve tossed with fresh baby spinach.

Cauliflower & Eggs Salad

Ingredients - Allergies: SF, GF, NF

- 2 cup chopped Cauliflower
- 4 hardboiled eggs - chopped,
- 4 oz. shredded cheddar cheese, low-fat
- 1 red onion, celery,
- 1 dill pickles,
- 1 tbsp. yellow mustard.

Mix all ingredients.

Quinoa & Almond Superfoods Tabbouleh

Ingredients - Allergies: SF, GF, EF

- 2 cups cooked quinoa
- 1 bunch mint, leaves picked & 1 bunch flat leaf parsley
- 1/2 small red onion, finely chopped
- 1/4 Cup lemon juice & 1/4 Cup extra virgin olive oil
- 1/4 Cup whole almonds & 1/4 cup chia or sunflower seeds
- 1/2 Cup cherry tomatoes & 1 Avocado optional
- 1/2 Cup chopped Kale or Dandelion
- Low fat yogurt, to serve, optional

Instructions

Cook quinoa and let it cool. Chop off and discard half of the parsley stalks. Finely chop the remaining parsley bunch, mint and greens. Stir herbs in a salad bowl and add onion to drained quinoa. Combine lemon juice and olive oil and season well. Add other ingredients, mix and dress salad.

Greek Cucumber Salad

Ingredients - Allergies: SF, GF, EF, NF

- 2 cucumbers, sliced
- 1 teaspoon salt
- 2 tbsp. lemon juice
- 1/4 tsp. paprika
- 1/4 tsp. white pepper
- 1/2 clove garlic, minced
- 2 fresh green onions, diced
- 1 cup thick Greek Yogurt

- 1/4 tsp. paprika

Instructions

Slice cucumbers thinly, sprinkle with salt and mix. Set aside for one hour. Mix lemon juice, water, garlic, paprika and white pepper, and set aside. Squeeze liquid from cucumber slices a few at a time, and place slices in the bowl. Discard liquid. Add lemon juice mixture, green onions, and yogurt. Mix and sprinkle additional paprika or dill over top. Chill for 1-2 hours.

Mediterranean Salad

Ingredients - Allergies: SF, GF, DF, EF, V, NF

- 1 small head romaine lettuce, torn
- 1 tomato, diced
- 1 small cucumber, sliced
- 1/2 green bell pepper, sliced
- 1/2 small onion, cut into rings
- 3 radishes, thinly sliced
- 1/4 cup flat leaf parsley, chopped
- 1/4 cup olive oil or avocado oil
- 2 tbsp. lemon juice
- 1 garlic clove, minced
- Salt & pepper
- 1 tsp. fresh mint, minced

Instructions

Combine lettuce, tomatoes, cucumber, pepper, onion, radishes & parsley in a salad bowl. Whisk together olive oil, lemon juice, garlic, salt, pepper & mint. Pour over salad & toss to coat.

Pomegranate Avocado salad

Ingredients - Allergies: SF, GF, DF, EF, V

- 2 cups mixed greens, spinach, arugula, red leaf lettuce
- 1 ripe avocado, cut into 1/2-inch pieces
- 1 cup pomegranate seeds
- 1/2 cup pecan
- 1/2 cup blackberries
- 1/2 cup cherry tomatoes
- Olive oil, salt, lemon juice

Instructions

Combine greens, pecan, cut avocado, tomatoes, pomegranates and blackberries in a salad bowl. Whisk together salt, olive oil and lemon juice and pour over salad.

Roasted Beet Salad

Instructions - Allergies: SF, GF, DF, EF, V, NF

Toss 3 beets cut in half in a baking dish with olive oil, salt and pepper. Cover and roast at 425 degrees F until tender; let cool, then rub off the skins. Toss with any juices from the baking dish, capers, chopped pickles, a dash each of hot sauce, and chopped parsley or dill.

Apple Coleslaw

Ingredients - Allergies: SF, GF, DF, EF, V, NF

- 2 cups chopped cabbage (various color)
- 1 tart apple chopped
- 1 celery, chopped
- 1 red pepper chopped
- 4 tsp. olive oil or avocado oil
- juice of 1 lemon
- 1 Tbs. raw honey (optional)
- dash sea salt

Instructions

Toss the cabbage, apple, celery, and pepper together in a large bowl. In a smaller bowl, whisk remaining ingredients. Drizzle over coleslaw and toss to coat.

Chickpeas, Quinoa, Radish & Cucumber Salad

Serves 2

Ingredients - Allergies: SF, GF, DF, EF, NF, V

- 1 cup cooked quinoa
- 1/2 cup chopped cucumber
- 1/2 cup chopped radish
- 1 cup cooked chickpeas mixed with 1 tbsp. chia seeds
- 1/2 cup sliced leeks

Dressing:
- 1 tbsp. olive oil or black cumin oil
- 1 tbsp. fresh lemon juice
- pinch of black pepper
- pinch of sea salt
- 1 tbsp. hemp seeds

Instructions: Mix all ingredients.

Steak, Broccoli & Mushrooms Salad
Serves 2

Ingredients - Allergies: SF, GF, DF, EF, NF

- 2 grilled sirloin steaks
- 1 stir fried mushrooms
- 1 cup stir fried broccoli

Dressing:
- 1 tbsp. olive oil or avocado oil
- 1 tbsp. fresh lemon juice
- pinch of black pepper
- pinch of sea salt

Instructions: Mix all ingredients.

Arugula, Quinoa, Red Peppers & Almonds Salad

Serves 2

Ingredients - Allergies: SF, GF, DF, EF, V

- 1 cup cooked quinoa mixed with 1 tbsp. ground chia seeds
- 1/2 cup chopped red peppers
- 1/2 cup chopped almonds
- 1 cup arugula

Dressing:
- 1 tbsp. olive oil
- 1 tbsp. fresh lemon juice
- pinch of black pepper
- pinch of sea salt

Instructions: Mix all ingredients.

Pumpkin, Quinoa, Cheese & Arugula Salad

Serves 2

Ingredients - Allergies: SF, GF, EF, NF

- 1 cup cooked quinoa mixed with 1 tbsp. chia seeds
- 1/2 cup low fat feta cheese
- 1/2 cup chopped arugula
- 1 cup cooked Pumpkin, chopped

Dressing:
- 1 tbsp. olive oil or avocado oil
- 1 tbsp. fresh lemon juice
- pinch of black pepper
- pinch of sea salt
- 1 tbsp. hemp seeds

Instructions: Mix all ingredients.

Pear, Quinoa, Spinach & Grapes Salad

Serves 2

Ingredients - Allergies: SF, GF, DF, EF, NF, V

- 1 cup cooked quinoa mixed with 1 tbsp. sesame seeds
- 1/2 cup spinach
- 1/2 cup red grape seeds
- 1 cup chopped pear

Dressing:
- 1 tbsp. olive oil or black cumin oil
- 1 tbsp. fresh lemon juice
- pinch of black pepper
- pinch of sea salt

Instructions: Mix all ingredients.

Asparagus, Quinoa & Carrot Salad

Serves 2

Ingredients - Allergies: SF, GF, DF, EF, NF, V

- 1 cup cooked quinoa mixed with 1 tbsp. sunflower seeds
- 1/2 cup chopped carrots
- 1/2 cup chopped cucumbers
- 1 cup chopped asparagus
- 1/2 cup sliced green onions

Dressing:

- 1 tbsp. olive oil
- 1 tbsp. fresh lemon juice
- pinch of black pepper
- pinch of sea salt
- 2 lime quarters

Instructions: Mix all ingredients.

Pork, Red Quinoa, Carrot & Pumpkin Salad
Serves 2

Ingredients - Allergies: SF, GF, DF, EF, NF

- 1 cup cooked quinoa mixed with 1 tbsp. chia seeds
- 1/2 cup chopped pumpkin
- 1/2 cup chopped pork meat
- 1/2 cup chopped carrot
- 1/2 cup green peas

Dressing:
- 1 tbsp. olive oil
- 1 tbsp. fresh lemon juice
- pinch of black pepper
- pinch of sea salt
- 1 tbsp. hemp seeds

Instructions: Mix all ingredients.

Chicken, Roasted Veggies & Arugula Salad
Serves 2

Ingredients - Allergies: SF, GF, DF, EF, NF

- 1 cup sliced grilled chicken
- 1/2 cup tomato
- 1/2 cup grilled veggies
- 1 cup arugula
- 1/2 cup chopped red peppers

Dressing:
- 1 tbsp. olive oil or avocado oil
- 1 tbsp. fresh lemon juice
- pinch of black pepper
- pinch of sea salt

Instructions: Mix all ingredients.

Broccoli, Quinoa, Shrimps & Scallops Salad

Serves 2

Ingredients - Allergies: SF, GF, DF, EF, NF

- 1 cup cooked quinoa mixed with 1 tbsp. ground flax seeds
- 1 cup stir fried broccoli
- 1/2 cup green peas
- 1 cup stir fried shrimp and scallops

Dressing:
- 1 tbsp. olive oil
- 1 tbsp. fresh lemon juice
- pinch of black pepper
- pinch of sea salt

Instructions: Mix all ingredients.

Shrimp, Figs, Lettuce & Orange Salad
Serves 2

Ingredients - Allergies: SF, GF, DF, EF, NF

- 1 cup grilled shrimp
- 1/2 cup chopped figs
- 1/2 cup chopped orange
- 1 cup Lettuce
- 1/2 cup pomegranate seeds

Dressing:
- 1 tbsp. olive oil or avocado oil
- 1 tbsp. fresh lemon juice
- pinch of black pepper
- pinch of sea salt

Instructions: Mix all ingredients.

Appetizers

Hummus

Ingredients - Allergies: SF, GF, DF, EF, V, NF

- 1 cup cooked chickpeas (garbanzo beans)
- 1/8 cup (59 ml) fresh lemon juice, about 1 large lemon
- 1/4 cup (59 ml) tahini
- Half of a large garlic clove, minced
- 1 tbsp. olive oil or cumin oil, plus more for serving
- 1/2 tsp. salt
- 1/4 tsp. ground cumin
- 2 to 3 tbsp. water
- Dash of ground paprika for serving

Instructions

Combine tahini and lemon juice and blend for 1 minute. Add the olive oil, minced garlic, cumin and the salt to tahini and lemon mixture. Process for 30 seconds, scrape sides and then process 30 seconds more.

Add half of the chickpeas to the food processor and process for 1 minute. Scrape sides, add remaining chickpeas and process for 1 to 2 minutes.

Transfer the hummus into a bowl then drizzle about 1 tbsp. of olive oil over the top and sprinkle with paprika.

Guacamole

Ingredients - Allergies: SF, GF, DF, EF, V, NF

- 2 ripe avocados
- 2 tbsp. freshly squeezed lemon juice (1 lemon)
- 4 dashes hot pepper sauce
- 1/4 cup diced onion
- 1 garlic clove, minced
- 1/2 tsp. salt
- 1/2 tsp. ground black pepper
- 1 small tomato, seeded, and small-diced

Instructions

Cut the avocados in half, remove the pits, and scoop the flesh out. Immediately add the lemon juice, hot pepper sauce, garlic, onion, salt, and pepper and toss well. Dice avocados. Add the tomatoes. Mix well and taste for salt and pepper.

Baba Ghanoush

Ingredients - Allergies: SF, GF, DF, EF, V, NF

- 1 eggplant
- 1/4 cup tahini, plus more as needed
- 1 garlic clove, minced
- 1/8 cup fresh lemon juice, plus more as needed
- 1 pinch ground cumin
- salt, to taste
- 1 tbsp. extra-virgin olive oil or avocado oil
- 1 tbsp. chopped flat-leaf parsley
- 1/4 cup brine-cured black olives, such as Kalamata

Instructions:

Grill eggplant for 10 to 15 minutes. Heat the oven (375 F).

Put the eggplant to a baking sheet and bake 15-20 minutes or until very soft. Remove from the oven, let cool, and peel off and discard the skin. Put the eggplant flesh in a bowl. Using a fork, mash the eggplant to a paste.

Add the 1/4 cup tahini, garlic, cumin, 1/4 cup lemon juice and mix well. Season with salt to taste. Transfer the mixture to a serving bowl and spread with the back of a spoon to form a shallow well. Drizzle the olive oil over the top and sprinkle with the parsley.

Serve at room temperature.

Espinacase la Catalana

Ingredients - Allergies: SF, GF, DF, EF, V

- 1 cup spinach
- 1 cloves garlic
- 2 tbsp cashews
- 2 tbsp dried currants
- olive oil or avocado oil

Instructions

Wash the spinach and trim off the stems. Steam the spinach for few minutes.

Peel and slice the garlic. Pour a few tablespoons of olive oil and cover the bottom of a frying pan. Heat pan on medium and sauté garlic for 1-2 minutes. Add the cashews and the currants to the pan and continue to sauté for 1 minute. Add the spinach and mix well, coating with oil. Salt to taste.

Tapenade

Ingredients - Allergies: SF, GF, DF, EF, V, NF

- 1/4 pound olives with pit removed
- 2 anchovy fillets, rinsed
- 1 small clove garlic, minced
- 2 tbsp. capers
- 2 fresh basil leaves
- 1 tbsp. freshly squeezed lemon juice
- 1 tbsp. extra-virgin olive oil or cumin oil

Instructions

Rinse the olives in cool water. Place all ingredients in the bowl of a food processor. Process to combine, until it becomes a coarse paste. Transfer to a bowl and serve.

Red Pepper Dip

Ingredients - Allergies: SF, GF, EF, NF

- 1/2 pound red peppers
- 1/2 cup farmers' cheese
- 1 Tbsp. virgin olive oil or avocado oil
- 1/2 tbsp minced garlic
- Lemon juice, salt, basil, oregano, red pepper flakes to taste.

Instructions

Roast the peppers. Cover them and cool for about 15 minutes. Peel the peppers and remove the seeds and stems. Chop the peppers.
Transfer the peppers and garlic to a food processor and process until smooth. Add the farmers' cheese and garlic and process until smooth. With the machine running, add olive oil and lemon juice. Add the basil, oregano, red pepper flakes, and 1/8 tsp. salt, and process until smooth. Adjust the seasoning, to taste. Pour to a bowl and refrigerate.

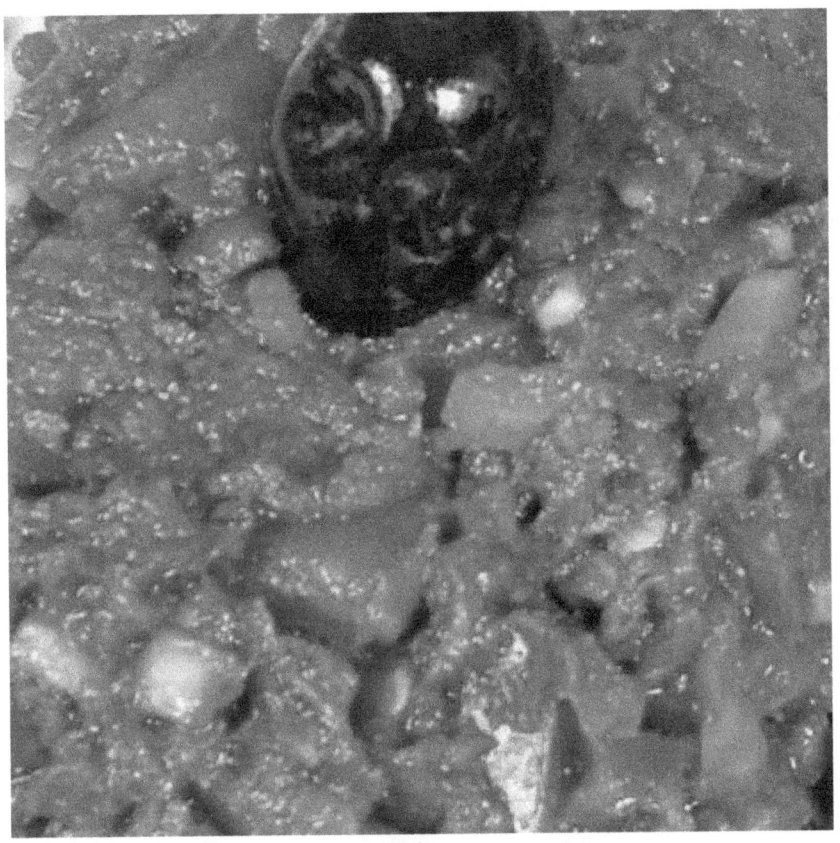

Roasted Garlic

Instructions - Allergies: SF, GF, DF, EF, V, NF

Heat the oven to 350 F.
Rub olive oil into the top of each garlic head and place it cut side down on a foil-lined baking sheet. Bake until the cloves turn golden. Remove from the oven and let cool. Squeeze each head of garlic to expel the cloves into a bowl. Mash into a paste.

Eggplant and Yogurt

Instructions - Allergies: SF, GF, EF, NF

Mix 1/2 pound chopped eggplant, 1 unpeeled shallot and 1 unpeeled garlic cloves with 1/8 cup olive oil, salt and pepper on a baking sheet. Roast at 400 degrees for half an hour. Cool and squeeze the shallots and garlic from their skins and chop. Mix with the eggplant, almond, 1/2 cup plain yogurt, dill and salt and pepper.

Caponata

Ingredients - Allergies: SF, GF, DF

- Coconut oil
- 1 large eggplants, cut into large chunks
- 1 tsp. dried oregano
- Sea salt
- Freshly ground black pepper
- 1 small onion, peeled and finely chopped
- 1 clove garlic, peeled and finely sliced
- 1 small bunch fresh flat-leaf parsley, leaves picked and stalks finely chopped
- 1 tbsp. salted capers, rinsed, soaked and drained
- 1 handful green olives, stones removed
- 2 tbsp. lemon juice
- 2 large ripe tomatoes, roughly chopped
- coconut oil
- 2 tbsp. slivered almonds, lightly toasted, optional

Instructions

Heat coconut oil in a pan and add eggplant, oregano and salt. Cook on a high heat for around 4 or 5 minutes. Add the onion, garlic and parsley stalks and continue cooking for another few minutes. Add drained capers and the olives and lemon juice. When all the juice has evaporated, add the tomatoes and simmer until tender.

Season with salt and olive oil to taste before serving. Sprinkle with almonds.

Soups

Cream of Broccoli Soup

Ingredients - Allergies: SF, GF, EF, NF

- 1 pound broccoli, fresh
- 1 cup water
- 1/4 tsp. salt, pepper to taste
- 1/4 cup tapioca flour, mixed with 1 cup cold water
- 1/4 cup coconut cream
- 1/4 cup low-fat farmers' cheese

Steam or boil broccoli until it gets tender.
Put 1 cup of water and coconut cream in top of double boiler.
Add salt, cheese and pepper. Heat until cheese gets melted.
Add broccoli. Mix water and tapioca flour in a small bowl.
Stir tapioca mixture into cheese mixture in double boiler and heat until soup thickens.

Lentil Soup

Ingredients - Allergies: SF, GF, DF, EF, NF
- 1 tbsp. olive oil or avocado oil
- 1/2 cup finely chopped onion
- 1/4 cup chopped carrot
- 1/4 cup chopped celery
- 1 teaspoons salt
- 1/2 pound lentils
- 1/2 cup chopped tomatoes
- 1 quart chicken or vegetable broth
- 1/4 tsp. ground coriander & toasted cumin

Instructions

Place the olive oil into a large Dutch oven. Set over medium heat. Once hot, add the celery, onion, carrot and salt and do until the onions are translucent. Add the lentils, tomatoes, cumin, broth and coriander and stir to combine. Increase the heat and bring just to a boil. Reduce the heat, cover and simmer at a low until the lentils are tender (approx. 35 to 40 minutes). Puree with a bender to your preferred consistency (optional). Serve immediately.

Cold Cucumber Avocado Soup

Ingredients - Allergies: SF, GF, EF, NF
- 1 cucumber peeled, seeded and cut into 2-inch chunks
- 1 avocado, peeled
- 1 chopped scallions
- 1 cup chicken broth
- 1/3 cup Greek low-fat yogurt
- 1 tbsp. lemon juice
- 1/4 tsp. ground pepper, or to taste

Garnish:
- Chopped chives, dill, mint, scallions or cucumber

Instructions
Combine the cucumber, avocado and scallions in a blender. Pulse until chopped.
Add yogurt, broth and lemon juice and continue until smooth.
Season with pepper and salt to taste and chill for 4 hours.
Taste for seasoning and garnish.

Bouillabaisse

Ingredients - Allergies: SF, GF, DF, EF, NF

- 1 pound of 3 different kinds of fish fillets
- 1/4 cup Coconut oil
- 1 pounds of Oysters, clams, or mussels
- 1/3 cup cooked shrimp, crab, or lobster meat, or rock lobster tails
- 1/3 cup thinly sliced onions
- 1 Shallot or the white parts of 1 leek, thinly sliced
- 1 cloves garlic, crushed
- 1 small tomato, chopped
- 1/2 sweet red pepper, chopped
- 2 stalks celery, thinly sliced
- 1-inch slice of fennel or 1/2 tsp. of fennel seed
- 1 sprigs fresh thyme or 1/4 tsp. dried thyme
- 1 bay leaf
- 1 whole cloves
- Zest of half an orange
- 1/4 tsp. saffron
- 1 teaspoons salt
- 1/4 tsp. ground black pepper
- 1/3 cup clam juice or fish broth
- 1 Tbps lemon juice
- 1/3 cup white wine

Instructions

In a large saucepan heat 1/8 cup of the coconut oil. When it is hot, add onions and shallots (or leeks). Sauté for a minute. Add crushed garlic, and sweet red pepper. Add celery, tomato, and fennel. Stir the vegetables until well coated. Add another 1/8 cup of coconut oil, bay leaf, thyme, cloves and the orange zest. Cook until the onion is golden. Cut fish fillets. Make them 2-inch pieces. Add 1 cup of water and the pieces of fish to the vegetable mixture. Bring to a boil, then reduce heat and let it simmer, uncovered, for about 10 minutes. Add clams, oysters or mussels (optional) and crabmeat, shrimp or lobster tails, cut into pieces. Add salt, saffron and pepper. Add lemon juice, clam juice, and white wine. Bring to a simmer again and cook for 5 minutes longer.

Gaspacho

Ingredients - Allergies: SF, GF, DF, EF, V, NF
- 1/4 cup of flax seeds meal
- 1 pound tomatoes, diced
- 1 red pepper or 1 green pepper, diced
- 1 small cucumber, peeled and diced
- 1 cloves of garlic, peeled and crushed
- ¼ cup extra virgin olive oil or cumin oil
- 1 tbsp. lemon juice
- Salt, to taste

Instructions
Mix the peppers, tomatoes and cucumber with the crushed garlic and olive oil in the bowl of a blender. Add flax meal to the mixture. Blend until smooth. Add salt and lemon juice to taste and stir well. Refrigerate. Serve with black olives, hard-boiled egg, cilantro, mint or parsley.

Italian Beef Soup

Ingredients - Allergies: SF, GF, DF, EF, NF

- 1/3 pound minced beef
- 1 clove garlic, minced
- 1 cups beef broth
- 1 large tomato
- 1/2 cup sliced carrots
- 1 cup cooked beans
- 1 small zucchini, cubed
- 1 cups spinach - rinsed and torn
- 1/8 tsp. black pepper
- 1/8 tsp. salt

Brown beef with garlic in a stockpot. Stir in broth, carrots and tomatoes. Season with salt and pepper. Reduce heat, cover, and simmer for 15 minutes.

Stir in beans with liquid and zucchini. Cover, and simmer until zucchini is tender. Remove from heat, add spinach and cover. Serve after 5 minutes.

Creamy roasted mushroom

Ingredients - Allergies: SF, GF, DF, EF, V, NF

- 1/2 pound Portobello mushrooms, cut into 1inch pieces
- 1/4 pound shiitake mushrooms, stemmed
- 2 tbsp. olive oil or avocado oil
- 1 cups vegetable broth
- 1 tbsp. coconut oil
- 1/2 onion, chopped
- 1 garlic cloves, minced
- 1 tbsp. arrowroot flour
- 1/4 cup coconut cream
- 1/4 tsp. chopped thyme

Instructions

Heat oven to 400°F. Line one large baking sheets with foil. Spread mushrooms and drizzle some olive oil on them. Season with salt and pepper and toss. Cover with foil and bake them for half an hour. Uncover and continue baking 15 minutes more. Cool slightly. Mix one half of the mushrooms with one can of broth in a blender. Set aside.

Melt coconut oil in a large pot over high heat. Add onion and garlic and sauté until onion is translucent. Add flour and stir 2 minutes. Add cream, broth, and thyme. Stir in remaining cooked mushrooms and mushroom puree. Simmer over low heat until thickened (approx. 10 minutes). Season to taste with salt and pepper.

Black Bean Soup

Ingredients - Allergies: SF, GF, DF, EF, NF

- 1 Tbsp. cup Coconut Oil
- 1/4 cup Onion, Diced
- 1/4 cup Carrots, Diced
- 1/4 cup Green Bell Pepper, Diced
- 1 cup beef broth
- 1 pound cooked Black Beans
- 1 tbsp. lemon juice
- 1 teaspoons chopped Garlic
- 1 teaspoons Salt
- 1/4 tsp. Black Pepper, Ground
- 1 teaspoons Chili Powder
- 4 oz. pork
- 1 tbsp. tapioca flour
- 2 tbsp. Water

Instructions

Place coconut oil, onion, carrot, and bell pepper in a stock pot. Cook the veggies until tender. Bring broth to a boil. Add cooked beans, broth and the remaining ingredients (except tapioca flour and 2 tbsp. water) to the vegetables. Bring that mixture to a simmer and cook approximately 15 minutes. Puree 1 quart of the soup in a blender and put back into the pot. Combine the tapioca flour and 2 tbsp. water in a separate bowl. Add the tapioca flour mixture to the bean soup and bring to a boil for 1 minute.

Ajoblanco con uvas - Almond and garlic soup-*White Gazpacho*

Ingredients - Allergies: SF, GF, DF, EF, V

- 1/2 cup flax seeds meal
- ½ cups almonds, blanched and skinned
- 1 cloves garlic
- 2 Tbsp. extra virgin olive oil or avocado oil
- 3 tbsp. lemon juice
- 1 tsp salt
- 1/2 liter water
- ½ cup grapes, seeded

Instructions

Put flax meal with the almonds and garlic in the blender. Blend to a smooth paste. Add a little bit of water if necessary. Add the oil in a slow stream with the motor running. Add the lemon juice and salt too. Pour the mixture into a pitcher and add the remaining water. Add salt or lemon juice to taste. Chill the soup. Stir before serving and garnish with grapes.

Squash soup

Ingredients - Allergies: SF, GF, DF, EF, V, NF

- 1 small squash
- 1 carrot, chopped
- 1/2 onion (diced)
- 1/2 cup coconut milk
- 1/4 cup water
- 1 tbsp. olive oil or avocado oil
- Salt
- Pepper
- Cinnamon
- Turmeric

Instructions

Cut the squash and spoon out the seeds. Cut it into large pieces and place on a baking sheet. Sprinkle with salt, olive oil, and pepper and bake at 375 degrees F until soft (approx. 1 hour). Let cool.

In the meantime, sauté the onions in olive oil (put it in a soup pot). Add the carrots. Add 1/4 cup coconut milk and 1/4 cup water after few minutes and let simmer. Scoop the squash out of its skin. Add it to the soup pot. Stir to combine the ingredients and let simmer a few minutes. Add more milk or water if needed. Season to taste with the salt, pepper and spices. Blend until smooth and creamy.

Sprinkle it with toasted pumpkin seeds.

Kale White Bean Pork Soup

Ingredients - Allergies: SF, GF, DF, EF, NF

- 1 tbsp. each extra-virgin olive oil and coconut oil
- 1 tbsp. chili powder
- 1/2 tbsp. jalapeno hot sauce
- 1/2 pound bone-in pork chops
- Salt
- 2 stalks celery, chopped
- 1 small white onion, chopped
- 1 cloves garlic, chopped
- 1 cup chicken broth
- 1 cups diced tomatoes
- 1 cup cooked white beans
- 2 cups packed Kale

Instructions

Preheat the broiler. Whisk hot sauce, 1 tbsp. olive oil and a pinch of chili powder in a bowl. Season the pork chops with 1/2 tsp. salt. Rub chops with the spice mixture on both sides and place them on a rack set over a baking sheet. Set aside.

Heat 1 tbsp. coconut oil in a large pot over high heat. Add the celery, garlic, onion and the remaining chili powder. Cook until onions are translucent, stirring (approx. 8 minutes).

Add tomatoes and the chicken broth to the pot. Cook and stir occasionally until reduced by about one-third (approx. 7 minutes). Add the kale and the beans. Reduce the heat to medium, cover and cook until the kale is tender (approx. 7 minutes). Add up to 1/2 cup water if the mixture looks dry and season with salt.

In the meantime, broil the pork until browned (approx. 4 to 6 minutes). Flip and broil until cooked through. Serve with the kale and beans.

Avgolemono – Greek lemon chicken soup

Ingredients - Allergies: SF, GF, DF, EF, NF
- 2 cups chicken broth
- 1/4 cup uncooked quinoa
- salt and pepper
- 2 eggs
- 2 tbsp. lemon juice
- Handful fresh dill (chopped)
- shredded roasted chicken (optional)

Bring the broth to a boil in a saucepan. Add the quinoa and cook until tender. Season with the salt and pepper. Reduce heat to low and let simmer. In a separate bowl, whisk lemon juice and the eggs until smooth. Add about 1 cup of the hot broth into the egg/lemon mixture and whisk to combine.

Add the mixture back to the saucepan. Stir until the soup becomes opaque and thickens. Add dill, salt and pepper. Optionally add chicken and serve.

Egg-Drop Soup

Ingredients - Allergies: SF, GF, DF, NF

- 2 cups quarts chicken broth
- 1 tbsps. Tapioca flour, mixed in 1/4 cup cold water
- 2 eggs, slightly beaten with a fork
- 2 scallions, chopped, including green ends

Instructions

Bring broth to a boil. Slowly pour in the tapioca flour mixture while stirring the broth. The broth should thicken. Reduce heat and let it simmer. Mix in the eggs very slowly while stirring. As soon as the last drop of egg is in, turn off the heat. Serve with chopped scallions on top.

Creamy Tomato Basil Soup

Ingredients - Allergies: SF, GF, DF, EF, V, NF

- 2 tomatoes - peeled, seeded and diced
- 2 cups tomato juice*
- 5 leaves fresh basil
- 1/2 cup coconut cream
- salt to taste
- ground black pepper to taste

Instructions

Combine tomatoes and tomato juice in stock pot. Simmer 30 minutes. Puree mixture with basil leaves in a processor. Put back in a stock pot and add coconut cream. Add salt and pepper to taste.

Minestrone

Ingredients - Allergies: SF, GF, DF, EF, NF

- 1 tbsp. coconut oil
- 1 cloves garlic, chopped
- 1/2 onions, chopped
- 1/2 cups chopped celery
- 2 carrots, sliced
- 1 cup chicken broth
- 1/2 cups water
- 1 cup tomato sauce
- 1/2 oz. red wine (optional)
- 1/2 cup cooked kidney beans
- 1/2 cups green beans
- 1/2 cups baby spinach, rinsed
- 1 small zucchinis, quartered and sliced
- 1/2 tbsp. chopped oregano
- 1 tbsp. chopped basil
- salt and pepper to taste
- 1/2 tbsp. olive oil or cumin oil

Instructions

Heat coconut oil over medium heat in a stock pot, and sauté garlic for few minutes. Add onion and sauté for few more minutes. Add celery and carrots and sauté for 2 minutes.
Add chicken broth, tomato sauce and water and bring to boil, stirring frequently. Add red wine at this point. Reduce heat to low and add kidney beans, zucchini, green beans, spinach leaves, oregano, basil, salt and pepper. Simmer for 30 to 40 minutes.

Grilled Meats & Salad

Chicken and Large Fiber Loaded Salad with Italian Dressing

Allergies: SF, GF, EF, NF

• 2 6oz. pieces of Chicken (or turkey), skinless, boneless grilled or prepared in the skillet.

• Large mixed spinach and lettuce salad with Italian Dressing and half a tsp of mustard. Salad can be as large as you want, but use half a cup of the dressing.

Salmon with Large Fiber Loaded Salad with Italian Dressing

Allergies: SF, GF, DF, EF, NF

- 2 Salmon steaks grilled or prepared in the skillet.

- Large mixed spinach and lettuce salad with "Italian Dressing" and some thyme sprinkled on top of it. Salad can be as large as you want, but use the prescribed amount of the dressing.

Ground Beef Patty with Large Fiber Loaded Salad with Yogurt Dressing

Allergies: SF, GF, EF, NF

- 2 5oz. lean ground beef patty grilled or prepared in the skillet.
- Large mixed spinach and shredded cabbage salad with Yogurt Dressing. Salad can be as large as you want, but use half a cup of a dressing.

Lean Pork with Fiber Loaded Salad with Yogurt Dressing

Allergies: SF, GF, EF, NF

- 2 5oz. lean Pork Tenderloin pieces grilled or prepared in the skillet.
- Large mixed spinach and shredded cabbage salad with Yogurt Dressing and half a tsp of mustard. Salad can be as large as you want, but use half a cup of the dressing.

Caribbean Chicken salad

Ingredients - Allergies: SF, GF, DF, EF, NF

- 2 boneless skinless chicken breasts

Marinade

- 1/2 cup fish sauce
- 2 tomatoes (seeded and chopped)
- 1/2 cup chopped onion
- 2 tsps. jalapeno chilies (minced)
- 2 tsps. chopped cilantro fresh

Raw honey Lime Dressing:

- 1/4 cup mustard
- 1/4 cup raw honey
- 1 tbsp coconut oil
- 1 1/2 tbsps. lemon juice
- 1 1/2 tsps. lime juice
- 3/4 lb mixed greens

Instructions

Blend all the marinade ingredients in a small bowl with a hand blender. Cover and chill. Marinate the chicken for at least two hours in the fridge. Grill the chicken for few minutes per side or until done.

Serve the greens into 2 large salad bowls.
Slice the chicken into thin strips. Divide among bowls.
Pour the dressing aside and serve with the salads.

Herb Crusted Salmon

Allergies: SF, GF, DF, EF, NF

Rub some tarragon, chives and parsley over 2 salmon steaks and add some salt and pepper. Heat the pan with 1 tsp of coconut oil to medium high and place the salmon, skin-side up in the pan. Cook until golden brown on 1 side, about 4 minutes. Turn the fish over and cook until it feels firm to the touch. Salmon is done when it flakes easily with a fork. Serve with a wedge of lemon.

• Large mixed spinach and lettuce salad with "Italian Dressing" and some thyme sprinkled on top of it. Salad can be as large as you want, but use the prescribed amount of the dressing.

Tuna with Large Fiber Loaded Salad with Italian Dressing

Allergies: SF, GF, DF, EF, NF

- 2 6oz. can of Tuna, drained.

- Large mixed spinach and green onion salad with Italian Dressing and half a tsp of mustard. Salad can be as large as you want, but use only the prescribed amount of dressing. You may use fish sauce instead of salt.

Stews, Chilies and Curries

Stuffed Peppers with beans

Ingredients - Allergies: SF, GF, DF, EF, V, NF

2 large red or green bell peppers
1 cup stewed tomatoes
1/3 cup brown rice
2 tbsp. hot water
2 green onions
8 ounces cooked black beans
1/4 tsp. crushed red pepper flakes

Instructions

Discard seeds and membrane from peppers. Place cut-side down and cover. Bake at 375F for 15 minutes.
While the peppers are cooking, cook tomatoes, rice and water for 15 minutes. In the meantime, thinly slice green onions.
Stir beans, green onions, and pepper flakes into tomato mixture. Cook for 10 minutes more. Drain peppers. Turn cut-side up. Spoon beans mixture evenly into peppers and bake in the oven for 5-10 minutes.

Vegetarian Chili

Ingredients - Allergies: SF, GF, DF, EF, V, NF

1 tbsp. coconut oil
1/2 cup chopped onions
1/2 cup chopped carrots
1 cloves garlic, minced
1/2 cup chopped green bell pepper
1/2 cup chopped red bell pepper
1/4 cup chopped celery
1/2 tbsp. chili powder
1/2 cups chopped mushrooms
1 cup chopped tomatoes
1 cups cooked kidney beans
1/2 tbsp. ground cumin
1/2 teaspoons oregano
1/2 teaspoons crushed basil leaves

Instructions

Heat coconut oil in a large saucepan and add onions, carrots and garlic; sauté until tender. Stir in green pepper, red pepper, celery and chili powder.
Cook, stirring often, until vegetables are tender, about 6 minutes. To the vegetables add mushrooms; cook 4 minutes. Stir in tomatoes, kidney beans, corn, cumin, oregano and basil. Bring to a boil. Reduce heat to medium. Cover and simmer for 20 minutes, stirring occasionally.

Lentil Stew

Ingredients - Allergies: SF, GF, DF, EF, NF

- 1 cup dry lentils
- 2 cups chicken broth
- 1 tomato
- 1 small potato chopped + 1/4 cup chopped carrot
- 1/4 cup chopped onion + 1/4 cup chopped celery (optional)
- few sprigs of parsley and basil + 1 garlic clove (minced)
- 1/2 pound of cubed lean pork or beef + pepper to taste

You can eat a salad of your choice with this stew.

Braised Green Peas with Beef

Ingredients - Allergies: SF, GF, DF, EF, NF

- 2 cups fresh or frozen green peas
- 1 onion, finely chopped
- 2 cloves of garlic, thinly sliced and 1/2 inch of peeled/sliced fresh ginger (if you like)
- 1/2 tsp. red pepper flakes, or to taste
- 1 tomato, roughly chopped
- 2 chopped carrots
- 2 tbsp. coconut oil
- 1 cup chicken broth
- 10 oz. cubed beef
- Salt and freshly ground black pepper

Heat the coconut oil in a skillet over medium heat. Sauté the onion, garlic and ginger until they are soft. Add the red pepper, carrot, and tomatoes and sauté until the tomato begins to soften. Add in the green peas. Add cubed lean beef. Add in the broth and simmer over medium heat. Cover and cook until the peas are tender. Season to taste with salt and pepper.

White Chicken Chili

Ingredients - Allergies: SF, GF, DF, EF, NF
- 2 large boneless, skinless chicken breasts
- 1 green bell peppers
- 1/2 yellow onion
- 1/2 jalapeno
- 1/4 cup diced green chilies (optional)
- 1/4 cup of spring onions
- 1 tbsp. coconut oil
- 1 cup cooked white beans
- 2 cups chicken or vegetable broth
- 1/2 tsp. ground cumin
- 1/8 tsp. cayenne pepper
- salt to taste

Instructions

Bring a pot of water to boil. Add the chicken breasts and cook until cooked through. Drain water and allow chicken to cool. When cool, shred and set aside.

Dice the bell peppers, jalapeno and onion. Melt the coconut oil in a pot over high heat. Add the peppers and onions and sauté until soft, approx. 8-10 minutes.

Add the broth, beans, chicken and spices to the pot. Stir and bring to a low boil. Cover and simmer for 25-30 minutes.

Simmer for 10 more minutes and stir occasionally. Remove from heat. Let stand for 10 minutes to thicken. Top with cilantro.

Kale Pork

Ingredients - Allergies: SF, GF, DF, EF, NF

- 1 tbsp. coconut oil
- 1/2 pound pork tenderloin, trimmed and cut into 1-inch pieces
- 1/4 tsp. salt
- 1/2 medium onion, finely chopped
- 2 cloves garlic, minced
- 1 teaspoons paprika
- 1/8 tsp. crushed red pepper (optional)
- 1/2 cup white wine
- 2 plum tomatoes, chopped
- 2 cups chicken broth
- 1/2 bunch kale, chopped
- 1 cups cooked white beans

Instructions

Heat oil in a pot over medium heat. Add pork, season with salt and cook until no longer pink. Transfer to a plate and leave juices in the pot.

Add onion to the pot and cook until turns translucent. Add paprika, garlic and crushed red pepper and cook about 30 seconds. Add tomatoes and wine, increase heat and stir to scrape up any browned bits. Add broth. Bring to a boil.

Add kale and stir until it wilts. Lower the heat and simmer, until the kale is tender. Stir in beans, pork and pork juices. Simmer for 2 more minutes.

30-Minute Squash Cauliflower and Green Peppers Coconut Curry

Ingredients - Allergies: SF, GF, DF, EF, V, NF

- Curry Paste
- 1 cups peeled, chopped squash
- 1 cup thick coconut milk
- 1 tbsp. coconut oil
- 1 tbsp. raw honey
- 1 pound tomatoes
- 1/2 cup brown rice, uncooked
- 1/2 cup chopped Cauliflower
- 1/2 cup chopped Green Peppers
- Cilantro for topping

Instructions

Cook brown rice. Set aside.

Make Curry Paste. Pour the coconut milk into the skillet and mix the curry and raw honey into the coconut milk. Add the cauliflower, squash, and green peppers. Cover and simmer until squash is tender. Remove from heat and let stand for 10 minutes. The sauce will thicken.

Serve the curry over brown rice. Add chopped cilantro before serving.

Crockpot Red Curry Lamb

Ingredients - Allergies: SF, GF, DF, EF, NF

- 1/2 pounds cubed lamb meat
- Curry Paste *
- 1/2 cups tomato paste
- 1 tsp. salt
- 1/4 cup coconut milk or cream

Instructions

Make the Curry Paste. Add lamb and the curry paste in a crockpot. Pour half a cup of tomato paste over the lamb. Add 1/4 cups of water to the crockpot. Stir, cover and cook on high for 2 hours or low for 4-5 hours. Taste and season with salt.

Stir in the coconut milk and sprinkle with cilantro before serving. Serve over brown rice or naan bread.

Easy Lentil Dhal

Ingredients - Allergies: SF, GF, DF, EF, V, NF

- 1 cup lentils
- 1 cup of water
- Curry Paste *
- 1/4 cup coconut milk
- 1/4 cup water
- 1/4 teaspoons salt + 1/8 tsp. black pepper
- lime juice
- Cilantro and spring onions for garnish

Instructions

Bring the water to a boil in a large pot. Add lentils and cook uncovered for 10 minutes, stirring frequently. Remove from heat. Stir in remaining ingredients. Season with salt and herbs for garnish.

Gumbo

Ingredients - Allergies: SF, GF, DF, EF, NF

- 1/4 pound medium shrimp peeled
- 1/4 pound skinless, boneless chicken breasts, cut bite size
- 1 Tbsp. coconut oil
- 1 Tbsp. almond flour
- 1/2 cups chopped onions
- 1/4 cup chopped celery
- 1/4 cup chopped green pepper
- 1/4 tsp. ground cumin
- 1/4 tbsp. minced fresh garlic
- 1/4 tsp. fresh thyme chopped
- 1/8 tsp. red pepper
- 1 cup chicken broth
- 1/2 cups diced tomatoes
- 1/2 cups sliced okra
- 1/4 cup fresh parsley chopped
- 1 bay leaf
- 1/4 tsp. hot sauce

Instructions

Sauté' chicken on high heat until brown in a large pot. Remove and set aside. Chop onions, celery, and green pepper and set aside.

Place oil and flour in pot. Stir well and brown to make a roux. When roux is done add chopped vegetables. Sauté on low heat for 10 minutes.

Slowly add chicken broth stirring constantly.

Add chicken and all other ingredients except the okra, shrimp and parsley, which will be saved for the end.

Cover and simmer on low for half an hour. Remove lid and cook for half an hour more, stirring occasionally.

Add shrimp, okra and parsley. Continue to cook on low heat uncovered for 15 minutes.

Chickpea Curry

Ingredients - Allergies: SF, GF, DF, EF, V, NF

- Curry Paste
- 2 cups cooked chickpeas
- 1/2 cup chopped cilantro

Instructions

Make Curry Paste. Mix in chickpeas and their liquid. Continue to cook and stir until all ingredients are well blended. Remove from heat. Stir in cilantro just before serving, reserving 1 tbsp. for garnish.

Red Curry Chicken

Ingredients - Allergies: SF, GF, DF, EF, NF

- 1 cup cubed chicken meat
- Curry Paste
- 2/3 cups tomato paste
- 2 Tbsp. coconut milk or cream
- Cilantro for garnishing
- Brown rice for serving

Instructions

Make Curry Paste. Add the tomato paste; stir and simmer until smooth. Add the chicken and the cream. Stir to combine. Simmer for 20 minutes. Serve with brown rice and cilantro.

Braised Green Beans with Pork

Ingredients - Allergies: SF, GF, DF, EF, NF

- 2 cups fresh or frozen green beans
- 1 onion, finely chopped
- 2 cloves of garlic, thinly sliced
- 1/2 inch of peeled/sliced fresh ginger
- 1/2 tsp. red pepper flakes, or to taste
- 2 tomatoes, roughly chopped
- 2 tbsp. coconut oil
- 1 cup chicken broth
- Salt and ground black pepper
- 1/4 lemon, cut into wedges, to serve
- 10 oz. lean pork

Instructions

Cut each bean in half. Heat the coconut oil in a skillet over medium heat. Sauté the onion, garlic and ginger over medium heat until they are soft. Add the red pepper and tomatoes and sauté until the tomato begins to break down. Stir in the green beans. Add cubed lean pork. Add broth and bring to a simmer over medium heat. Cover and cook for so long that the beans get tender. Season to taste with salt and pepper. Serve with wedge of lemon on the side.

Ratatouille

Ingredients - Allergies: SF, GF, DF, EF, V, NF

- 1 large eggplants
- 2 small zucchinis
- 1 medium onions
- 1 red or green peppers
- 2 large tomatoes
- 1 cloves garlic, crushed
- 2 tbsp. coconut oil
- 1/2 tbsp. fresh basil
- Salt and freshly milled black pepper

Instructions

Cut eggplant and zucchini into 1 inch slices. Then cut each slice in half. Salt them and leave them for one hour. The salt will draw out the bitterness.
Chop peppers and onions. Skin the tomatoes by boiling them for few minutes. Then quarter them, take out the seeds and chop the flesh. Fry garlic and the onions in the coconut oil in a saucepan for a 10 minutes. Add the peppers. Dry the eggplant and zucchini and add them to the saucepan. Add the basil, salt and pepper. Stir and simmer for half an hour.
Add the tomato flesh, check the amount of seasoning and cook for an additional 15 minutes with the lid off.

Barbecued Beef

Ingredients - Allergies: SF, GF, DF, EF, NF
- 1/2 cups tomato paste
- 1 Tbsp. lemon juice
- 1/2 tbsp. mustard
- 1/8 tsp. salt
- 1 chopped carrot
- 1/8 tsp. ground black pepper
- 1/4 tsp. minced garlic
- 1 pound boneless chuck roast

Instructions

In a large bowl, combine tomato paste, lemon juice and mustard. Stir in salt, pepper and garlic.
Place beef and carrot in a slow cooker. Pour tomato mixture over chuck roast. Cover, and cook on low for 7 to 9 hours.
Remove chuck roast from slow cooker, shred with a fork, and return to the slow cooker. Stir meat to evenly coat with sauce. Continue cooking approximately 1 hour.

Beef Tenderloin with Roasted Shallots

Ingredients - Allergies: SF, GF, DF, EF

- 1/2 pound shallots, halved lengthwise and peeled
- 1/2 tbsp. olive oil or avocado oil
- salt and pepper to taste
- 1 cup beef broth
- 1/4 cup red wine
- 1/2 teaspoons tomato paste
- 1 pound beef tenderloin roast, trimmed
- 1/4 tsp. dried thyme
- 1 tbsp. coconut oil
- 1/2 tbsp. almond flour

Instructions

Heat oven to 375 degrees F. Toss shallots with olive oil to coat in a baking pan and season with salt and pepper. Roast until shallots are tender, stirring occasionally, about half an hour.
Combine wine and beef broth in a sauce pan and bring to a boil. Cook over high heat. Volume should be reduced by half. Add in tomato paste. Set aside.
Pat beef dry and sprinkle with salt and thyme and pepper. Add beef to pan oiled with coconut oil. Brown on all sides over high heat.
Put pan back to the oven. Roast beef about half an hour for medium rare. Transfer beef to platter. Cover loosely with foil. Place pan on stove top and add broth mixture. Bring to boil and stir to scrape up any browned bits. Transfer to a different saucepan, and bring to simmer. Mix 1 1/2 tbsp. coconut oil and flour in small bowl and mix. Whisk into broth, and simmer until

sauce thickens. Stir in roasted shallots. Season with salt and pepper.

Cut beef into 1/2 inch thick slices. Spoon some sauce over.

Chili

Ingredients - Allergies: SF, GF, DF, EF, NF

- 1 tbsp. coconut oil
- 1 onion, chopped
- 1 cloves garlic, minced
- 1/4 pound ground beef
- 1/4 pound beef sirloin, cubed
- 1 cup diced tomatoes
- 1/4 cup strong brewed coffee
- 1/3 cup tomato paste
- 1 cups beef broth
- 1/4 tbsp. cumin seeds
- 1/4 tbsp. unsweetened cocoa powder
- 1/4 tsp. dried oregano
- 1/4 tsp. ground cayenne pepper
- 1/4 tsp. ground coriander
- 1/4 tsp. salt
- 1 1/2 cups cooked kidney beans
- 1 fresh hot chili peppers, chopped

Instructions

Heat oil in a saucepan over medium heat. Cook garlic, onions, sirloin and ground beef in oil until the meat is browned and the onions are translucent.
Mix in the diced tomatoes, coffee, tomato paste and beef broth. Season with oregano, cumin, cocoa powder, cayenne pepper, coriander and salt. Stir in hot chile peppers and 3 cups of the beans. Reduce heat to low, and simmer for two hours.

Stir in the 3 remaining cups of beans. Simmer for another 30 minutes.

Glazed Meatloaf

Ingredients - Allergies: SF, GF, DF, NF

- 1/4 cup tomato paste
- 1 Tbsp. lemon juice, divided
- 1/2 tsp. mustard powder
- 1 pounds ground beef
- 1/2 cup flax seeds meal
- 1/4 cup chopped onion
- 1 egg, beaten

Instructions

Heat oven to 350 degrees F. Combine mustard, tomato paste, 1/2 tbsp. lemon juice in a small bowl.
Combine onion, ground beef, flax, egg and remaining lemon juice in a separate larger bowl. And add 1/3 of the tomato paste mixture from the smaller bowl. Mix all well and place in a loaf pan.
Bake at 350 degrees F for one hour. Drain any excess fat and coat with remaining tomato paste mixture. Bake for 10 more minutes.

Eggplant Lasagna

Ingredients - Allergies: SF, GF, NF

- 1 large eggplant, peeled and sliced lengthwise into strips
- coconut oil
- salt and pepper

Meat Sauce

- 1/2 lbs ground sirloin or 1/2 lbs turkey breast
- 1 tbsp. coconut oil
- 1 onion, chopped
- 1 cloves chopped garlic
- 1/2 red pepper, chopped
- 8 ounce sliced mushrooms
- 1/2 tbsp. of oregano, basil and thyme each
- 1/2 tsp. fennel seed (optional)
- salt and pepper
- 1/2 tsp. red pepper flakes (optional)
- 1 cup chopped spinach
- 2 cups tomato sauce
- 1 cup diced tomatoes

Cheese Mixture

- 1 cup low-fat farmers cheese
- 1 egg
- 1 green onions, chopped

- 1/4 cup shredded low-fat mozzarella cheese (optional)

Instructions

Heat oven to 425 degrees.

Oil cookie sheet and arrange eggplant slice. Sprinkle with salt and pepper. Bake slices 5 minutes on each side. Lower oven temp to 375.

Brown onion, meat and garlic in coconut oil for 5 minutes. Add mushrooms and red pepper, and cook for 5 minutes. Add tomatoes, spinach and spices and simmer for 5-10 minutes.

Blend farmers' cheese, egg and onion mixture. Spread one third of meat sauce in bottom of a glass pan. Layer one half of eggplant slices and one half farmers' cheese. Repeat. Add last layer of sauce and then mozzarella on top.

Cover with foil. Bake at 375 degrees for one hour. Remove foil and bake until cheese is browned. Let it rest 10 minutes before serving.

Stuffed Eggplant

Serves – one half of eggplant per person

Allergies: SF, GF, DF, EF, NF

Rinse the eggplants. Cut off a slice from one end. Make a wide slit and salt them. Deseed tomatoes. Chop them finely. Cut the onions in thin slices. Chop the garlic cloves. Place them in a frying pan with coconut oil. Add the tomatoes, salt parsley, cumin, pepper, hot peppers and ground beef. Sauté for 10 minutes.

Squeeze eggplants, so the bitter juice goes out. Fill the wide slit with the ground beef mix. Pour the remaining mix over. Heat the oven to 375F in the meantime. Place eggplants a baking pan. Sprinkle them with olive oil, lemon juice and 1 cup of water. Cover the pan with a foil.

Stuffed Red Peppers with Beef

Ingredients - Allergies: SF, GF, DF, EF, NF

- 3 red bell peppers
- salt to taste
- 1/2 pound ground beef
- 1/4 cup chopped onion
- salt and pepper to taste
- 1 cup chopped tomatoes
- 1/4 cup uncooked brown rice or quinoa
- 1/4 cup water
- 1 cup tomato soup
- water as needed

Instructions

Bring a pot of salted water to a boil. Cut the tops off the peppers. Remove the seeds. Cook peppers in boiling water for 5 minutes and drain.
Sprinkle salt inside each pepper, and set aside.
In a skillet, sauté onions and beef until beef is browned. Drain off excess fat. Season with salt and pepper. Stir in rice, tomatoes and 1/2 cup water. Cover, and simmer until rice is tender. Remove from heat. Stir in the cheese.
Heat the oven to 350 degrees F. Stuff each pepper with the rice and beef mixture. Place peppers open side up in a baking dish. Combine tomato soup with just enough water to make the soup a gravy consistency in a separate bowl. Pour over the peppers.
Bake covered for 25 to 35 minutes.

Superfoods Goulash

Ingredients - Allergies: SF, GF, DF, EF, NF

- 1 1/2 cups cauliflower
- 1/2 pound ground beef
- 1 small onion, chopped
- salt to taste
- ground black pepper to taste
- garlic to taste
- 1 cup cooked kidney beans
- 1/2 cup tomato paste

Brown the ground beef and onion in a skillet, over medium heat. Drain off the fat. Add garlic, salt and pepper to taste.
Stir in the cauliflower, kidney beans and tomato paste. Cook until cauliflower is done.

Frijoles Charros

Ingredients - Allergies: SF, GF, DF, EF, NF

- 1/2 pound dry pinto beans
- 1 clove garlic, chopped
- 1/2 tsp. salt
- 1/4 pound pork, diced
- 1/2 onion, chopped & 2 fresh tomatoes, diced
- few sliced sliced jalapeno peppers
- 1/4 cup chopped cilantro

Instructions

Place pinto beans in a slow cooker. Cover with water. Mix in garlic and salt. Cover, and cook 1 hour on High.

Cook the pork in a skillet over high heat until brown. Drain the fat. Place onion in the skillet. Cook until tender. Mix in jalapenos and tomatoes. Cook until heated through. Transfer to the slow cooker and stir into the beans. Continue cooking for 4 hours on Low. Mix in cilantro about half an hour before the end of the cook time.

HEALTHY EATING FOR TWO

Chicken Cacciatore

Ingredients - Allergies: SF, GF, DF, EF, NF

- 1 pound of chicken thighs, with skin on
- 1 Tbsp. extra virgin olive oil or avocado oil
- Salt
- 1 small sliced onion
- 1/4 cup red wine
- 1 sliced red or green bell pepper
- 2 ounces sliced cremini mushrooms
- 1 sliced garlic cloves
- 1 cup peeled and chopped tomatoes
- 1/2 tsp. ground black pepper
- 1/2 tsp. dry oregano
- 1/2 tsp. dry thyme
- 1/2 sprig fresh rosemary
- 1/2 tbsp. fresh parsley

Instructions
Pat the chicken on all sides with salt. Heat the olive oil in a skillet on medium. Brown few chicken pieces skin side down in the pan (don't overcrowd) for 5 minutes, then turn. Set aside. Make sure you have 1 tbsp. of the rendered fat left.
Add the onions, mushrooms and bell peppers to the pan. Increase the heat to medium high. Cook until the onions are tender, stirring, about 10 minutes. Add the garlic and cook a minute more.
Add the wine. Scrape up any browned bits and simmer until the wine is reduced by half. Add the tomatoes, pepper, oregano, thyme and a tsp. of salt. Simmer uncovered for maybe 5 more minutes. Put the chicken pieces on top of the tomatoes, skin side up. Lower the heat. Cover the skillet with the lid slightly ajar.

Cook the chicken on a low simmer. Turning and baste from time to time. Add rosemary and cook until the meat is tender, about 30 to 40 minutes. Garnish with parsley.

Cabbage Stewed with Meat

Ingredients - Allergies: SF, GF, DF, EF, NF

- 1 pound ground beef
- 1/2 cup beef stock
- 1 small chopped onion
- 1 bay leaf
- 1/8 tsp. pepper
- 1 sliced celery ribs
- 2 cups shredded cabbage
- 1 carrot, sliced
- 1/2 cup tomato paste
- 1/4 tsp. salt

Instructions

Brown ground meat in a pot. Add beef stock, onion, pepper and bay leaf. Cover and simmer until tender (approx.. 30 minutes). Add celery, cabbage and carrot.

Cover and simmer until vegetables are tender. Mix in tomato paste and seasoning blend. Simmer uncovered for 20 minutes.

Beef Stew with Peas and Carrots

Ingredients - Allergies: SF, GF, DF, EF, NF

- 1/2 cup chopped carrots
- 1/8 cup chopped onions
- 1 tbsp. coconut oil
- 1 cup green peas
- 1 cups beef stock
- 1/4 tsp. salt
- 1/8 tsp. ground black pepper
- 1/4 tsp. minced garlic
- 1 pound boneless chuck roast

Instructions

Cook the onions in coconut oil on medium until they are tender (few minutes). Add all other ingredients and stir. Cover and cook on low heat for 2 hours. Mix almond flour with some cold water, add to the stew and cook for another minute.

Green Chicken Stew

Ingredients - Allergies: SF, GF, DF, EF, NF

- 1 cups broccoli florets
- 1/4 cup chopped celery stalks
- 1/4 cup sliced leeks
- 1 tbsp. coconut oil
- 1/2 cups green peas
- 1 cups chicken stock
- 1/4 tsp. salt
- 1/8 tsp. ground black pepper
- 1/4 tsp. minced garlic
- 1 pounds boneless skinless chicken pieces

Instructions

Cook the leeks in coconut oil on medium until they are tender (few minutes). Add all other ingredients and stir. Cover and cook on low heat for 1 hour. Mix almond flour with some cold water, add to the stew and cook for another minute.

Irish Stew

Ingredients - Allergies: SF, GF, DF, EF, NF

- 1 small chopped onions
- 1 Tbsp. coconut oil
- 1 sprig dried thyme
- 1 pound chopped meat from lamb neck
- 2 chopped carrots
- 1 tbsp. brown rice
- 1 ½ cup chicken stock
- Salt
- Ground black pepper
- 1 bouquet garni (thyme, parsley and bay leaf)
- 1 chopped sweet potatoes
- 1/2 bunch chopped parsley
- 1/2 bunch chives

Instructions

Cook the onions in coconut oil on medium until they are tender. Add the dried thyme and lamb and stir. Add brown rice, carrots and chicken stock. Add salt, pepper and bouquet garni. Cover and cook on low heat for 2 hours. Place sweet potatoes on top of the stew and cook for 30 minutes until the meat is falling apart.

Garnish with parsley and chives.

HEALTHY EATING FOR TWO

Hungarian Pea Stew

Ingredients - Allergies: SF, GF, DF, EF, NF

- 1 & 1/2 cups green peas
- 1 pound cubed pork
- 1 tbsp olive oil or avocado oil
- 1 tbsp almond flour
- 1 tbsp chopped parsley
- 1/2 cup water
- 1/4 tsp salt
- 1/2 cup coconut milk
- 1/2 tsp coconut sugar

Instructions

Simmer the pork and green peas in the olive oil over medium heat until almost tender (approx. 10 minutes)

Add salt, chopped parsley, coconut sugar and almond flour, and cook for another minute.

Add water then milk and stir.

Cook for another 4 minutes over low heat, stirring occasionally.

Chicken Tikka Masala

Ingredients - Allergies: SF, GF, DF, EF, NF

- 1 pound chicken pieces, skinless, bone in
- 1 tbsp. toasted paprika
- 1 tbsp. toasted ground cumin
- 1/2 tsp. cayenne pepper
- 1 tbsp. toasted ground coriander seed
- 1 tsp. ground turmeric
- 3 chopped cloves garlic
- 1 tbsp. chopped fresh ginger
- 1/2 cups yogurt
- 1/4 cup lemon juice (4 to 6 lemons)
- 1/4 tsp. sea salt
- 1 tbsp. coconut oil
- 1/4 sliced onion
- 1 cups chopped tomatoes
- 1/4 cup chopped cilantro
- 1/4 cup coconut cream

Instructions

Score chicken deeply at 1-inch intervals with a knife. Place chicken in a large baking dish.

Combine coriander, cumin, paprika, turmeric, and cayenne in a bowl and mix. Set aside 3 tbsp. of this spice mixture. Combine remaining spice mixture with garlic garlic, yogurt, ginger, salt and lemon juice in a large bowl and combine. Pour marinade over chicken pieces and coat every surface (use hands). Refrigerate and marinate between 4 and 8 hours, turning occasionally.

Heat coconut oil in a large pot over medium-high heat and add remaining garlic and ginger. Add onions. Cook about 10 minutes, stirring occasionally. Add reserved spice mixture and cook until fragrant, about half a minute. Scrape up any browned bits from bottom of pan and add tomatoes and half of cilantro. Simmer for 15 minutes. Let cool slightly and puree.

Stir in coconut cream and remaining one quarter cup lemon juice. Season to taste with salt and set aside until chicken is cooked.

Cook chicken on a grill or under a broiler.

Remove chicken from bone and cut into rough bite-sized chunks. Add chicken chunks to pot of sauce. Bring to a simmer over medium heat and cook about 10 minutes.
Sprinkle with remaining cilantro and serve with brown rice or grilled naan.

Greek Beef Stew (Stifado)

Ingredients - Allergies: SF, GF, DF, EF, NF

- 2 pieces of veal or beef osso bucco
- 6 whole shallots, peeled
- 1 bay leaves
- 2 garlic cloves
- 3 sprigs rosemary
- 6 whole pimento
- 5 whole cloves
- 1/2 tsp ground nutmeg
- 1/2 cup olive oil or avocado oil
- 1/3 cup apple cider vinegar
- 1 tbsp. salt
- 2 cups tomato paste
- 1/4 tsp black pepper

Instructions

Mix vinegar and tomato paste and set aside. Place the meat, shallots, garlic and all spices in the pot.

Add the tomato paste, oil and vinegar. Cover the pot, bring to low boil and simmer on low for 2 hours. Do not open and stir, just shake the pot occasionally.

Serve with brown rice or maybe quinoa.

Meat Stew with Red Beans

Ingredients - Allergies: SF, GF, DF, EF, NF

- 1 tbsp. olive oil or avocado oil
- 1/4 chopped onion
- 1 pound lean cubed stewing beef
- 1 tsp. ground cumin
- 1 tsp. ground turmeric (optional)
- 1/4 tsp. ground cinnamon (optional)
- 1 cups water
- 1 tbsp. chopped fresh parsley
- 1 tbsp. snipped chives
- 1 cup cooked kidney beans
- 1/2 lemon, juice of
- 1/2 tbsp. almond flour
- salt and black pepper

Instructions

Sauté the onion in a pan with two tablespoons of the ive oil until tender.

Add beef and cook until meat is browned on all sides. Stir in turmeric, cinnamon (both optional) and cumin and cook for one minute. Add water and bring to a boil.

Cover and simmer over low heat for 45 minutes. Stir occasionally. Sauté parsley and chives with the remaining 1 tbsp. of olive oil for about 2 minutes and add this mixture to the beef. Add kidney beans and lemon juice and season with salt and pepper.

Stir in one tbsp. of almond flour mixed with a bit of water to thicken the stew. Simmer uncovered for half an hour until meat gets tender. Serve with brown rice.

Lamb and Sweet Potato Stew

Ingredients - Allergies: SF, GF, DF, EF, NF

- 1/2 cups tomato paste
- 1/8 cup lemon juice
- 1 tbsp. mustard
- 1/4 tsp. salt
- 1/8 tsp. ground black pepper
- 1/8 cup chunky almond butter
- 1 cup cubed sweet potatoes
- 1/4 tsp. minced garlic
- 1 pounds boneless chuck roast

Instructions

In a large bowl, combine tomato paste, lemon juice, almond butter and mustard. Stir in salt, pepper, garlic and cubed sweet potato.

Place chuck roast in a slow cooker. Pour tomato mixture over chuck roast. Cover, and cook on low for 7 to 9 hours.

Remove chuck roast from slow cooker, shred with a fork, and return to the slow cooker. Stir meat to evenly coat with sauce. Continue cooking approximately 1 hour.

Beef, Parsnip, Celery Stew

Serves 2

Ingredients - Allergies: SF, GF, DF, EF, NF

- 1 pound cubed beef meat
- 1 chopped onion
- 2 chopped carrots
- 1 Tbsp. coconut oil
- 1/2 sprig dried thyme
- 1 chopped parsnip
- 1 tbsp. brown rice
- 1 cup beef stock
- Salt
- Ground black pepper
- 1 Tbsp. chopped parsley

Instructions

Put all ingredients in the slow cooker and cook on low for 8 hours.

Chicken Mushrooms & Olives Stew

Serves 2

Ingredients - Allergies: SF, GF, DF, EF, NF

- 1 pounds chicken with skin on
- 1 chopped carrot
- 1 small chopped onion
- 1 tbsp. coconut oil
- 1/2 cup sliced mushrooms
- 1/4 cup chopped celery
- 1/4 cup black olives
- 1/4 tsp. salt
- 1/8 tsp. ground black pepper
- 1/4 tsp. minced garlic
- 1/4 cup fresh parsley

Instructions

Put all ingredients in the crockpot, cover and cook on low 6 hours.

Chicken Pasanda Curry

Serves: 2

Ingredients - Allergies: SF, GF, DF, EF, NF

- 1 cup cubed chicken meat
- Curry Paste, but go low on the heat
- 1 cups tomato paste
- 1/4 cup coconut milk or cream
- Cilantro for garnishing

Instructions

Make Curry Paste. Add the tomato paste, chicken and the cream. Stir to combine, add to crockpot and cook on low for 3 hours.

Osso Bucco & Garlic Stew

Serves 2

Ingredients - Allergies: SF, GF, DF, EF, NF

- 2 cloves garlic
- 1 small chopped onion
- 1 chopped carrot
- 1 chopped celery stalk
- 1 tbsp. coconut oil
- 3/4 cup beef stock
- 1/4 tsp. salt
- 1/8 tsp. ground black pepper
- 1 tsp. chopped parsley
- 1 pound osso bucco

Instructions

Put all ingredients in the slow cooker and cook on low for 8 hours.

Beef Meatballs with White Beans
Serves 2

Ingredients - Allergies: SF, GF, DF, EF, NF

- 3/4 pounds baked meatballs (see recipe in bonus chapter)
- 1 Tbsp. coconut oil
- 1 cups uncooked white navy beans
- 1 1/2 cups beef stock
- Salt
- Ground black pepper
- 1 small chopped onion
- 1 Tbsp. chopped parsley
- 1 chopped carrot

Instructions

Add all ingredients but meatballs and cook on high for 4 hours. Add meatballs and cook on low for 2 hours more. Garnish with parsley.

Duck Stew

Serves 2

Ingredients - Allergies: SF, GF, DF, EF, NF

- 1 Tbsp. olive oil
- 1/2 pound chopped duck meat (1/2 inch wide)
- 1/4 pound duck liver, sliced
- 1 chopped carrot
- 1 celery stalk, chopped
- 1 small chopped onions
- 1 garlic cloves, chopped
- 1 cup chicken broth
- 1/2 cup sliced shiitake mushrooms
- 2 Tbsp. cup cilantro

Instructions

Put all ingredients in the slow cooker and cook on low for 4 Hrs.

Pork, Zucchini, Pork, Tomato & Corn Stew

Serves 2

Ingredients - Allergies: SF, GF, DF, EF, NF

- 1/2 cups cooked corn
- 1/2 cup chopped onions
- 1 cup sliced zucchini
- 1/2 cups chopped tomato
- 2 tbsp. coconut oil
- 1 tbsp. chopped garlic
- 1 tsp. salt and 1/2 tsp. ground pepper
- 1 pounds cubed pork

Instructions

Put ingredients in the slow cooker. Cover, and cook on low for 7 to 9 hours.

Red Peppers Pork Curry

Serves 2

Ingredients - Allergies: SF, GF, DF, EF, NF

- 1 1/2 cups sliced red peppers
- 1 cups chopped onions
- 2 tbsp. coconut oil
- 1/4 cup curry paste*
- 1 pounds chopped pork meat

Instructions

Put ingredients in the slow cooker. Cover, and cook on low for 7 to 9 hours.

Beef Ratatouille

Serves 2

Ingredients - Allergies: SF, GF, DF, EF, NF

- 1 cup sliced zucchini
- 1/2 cup chopped onions
- 1/2 cups sliced eggplant
- 1 cup sliced red peppers (or tomato)
- 2 tbsp. coconut oil
- 1 tsp. chopped garlic
- 1 tsp. salt and 1/2 tsp. ground pepper
- 1 pounds cubed beef

Instructions

Put ingredients in the slow cooker. Cover, and cook on low for 7 to 9 hours.

Chicken, Green Peas and Red Peppers Stew

Serves 2

Ingredients - Allergies: SF, GF, DF, EF, NF

- 1 cups green peas
- 1/2 cup chopped onions
- 1/2 cups sliced red peppers
- 2 tbsp. coconut oil
- 1 cups chicken broth
- 1 tsp. salt and 1/2 tsp. ground pepper
- 1 pounds cubed chicken

Instructions

Put ingredients in the slow cooker. Cover, and cook on low for 7 to 9 hours.

Crock Pot Turkey Roast Mediterranean style

Serves 2

Ingredients - Allergies: SF, GF, DF, EF, NF

- 1/4 cup Kalamata olives
- 1/4 cup chopped sun dried tomatoes
- 1/2 cup chicken broth
- 1 garlic clove, minced
- 1/2 cups chopped onions
- 2 tbsp. coconut oil
- 1 pounds turkey breast
- Rub thyme, salt and ground black pepper.

Instructions

Put ingredients in the slow cooker. Cover, and cook on low for 7 to 9 hours.

Slow Cooker Pot Roast

Serves 2

Ingredients - Allergies: SF, GF, DF, EF, NF

- 1/2 cup sliced celery
- 1/2 cup chopped carrot
- 1 cups beef broth
- ¼ cup red wine (optional) & 1 garlic clove (optional)
- 1/4 cup chopped onions
- 2 tbsp. coconut oil
- 1 pounds beef chuck roast
- Rub thyme, salt and ground black pepper. Add 1 bay leaf.

Instructions

Put ingredients in the slow cooker. Cover, and cook on low for 7 to 9 hours.

Black Bean, Chicken & Brown Rice Stew

Serves 2

Ingredients - Allergies: SF, GF, DF, EF, NF

- 1/2 cup brown rice
- 1/4 cup chopped onions
- 2 tbsp. coconut oil
- 1/2 cup uncooked black beans
- Salt, ground black pepper and ground cumin to taste
- 2 cup chicken stock
- 1 pounds chicken breast meat cut into stripes

Instructions

Put ingredients in the slow cooker. Cover, and cook on low for 7 to 9 hours.

Duck Curry

Serves 2

Ingredients - Allergies: SF, GF, DF, EF, NF

- 1/2 cup chopped onions
- 1/4 cup chopped carrots
- 1/2 cup chopped zucchini
- 1 tbsp. coconut oil
- 1 lb. duck meat
- Curry Paste, but go low on the heat
- 1/2 cups tomato paste
- 1/2 cup coconut milk or cream
- Cilantro for garnishing

Instructions

Make Curry Paste. Add the tomato paste, chicken, veggies and the cream. Stir to combine, add to crockpot and cook on low for 8 hours.

Eggplant Red Pepper Stew

Serves 2

Ingredients - Allergies: SF, GF, DF, EF, NF

- 1/2 cups chopped onions
- 1 tbsp. coconut oil
- Salt, ground black pepper to taste
- 1 pound cubed eggplant
- 1 cup sliced red peppers
- 1/2 tsp. dried red pepper flakes (to taste).
- 1/4 cup tomato paste.

Instructions

Put ingredients in the slow cooker. Cover, and cook on low for 8 hours.

Irish Lamb Stew

Serves 2

Ingredients - Allergies: SF, GF, DF, EF, NF

- 1/2 cups chopped onions
- 1 tbsp. coconut oil
- Salt, ground black pepper to taste
- 1 pound lamb neck meat
- 3/4 cup chopped sweet potato
- 1/2 cup chopped carrots
- 1/2 cup beef broth

Instructions

Put ingredients in the slow cooker. Cover, and cook on low for 8 hours.

Shrimp, Onion & Cilantro Stew
Serves 2

Ingredients - Allergies: SF, GF, DF, EF, NF

- 1 cup quartered onions
- 1 tbsp. coconut oil
- Salt, ground black pepper to taste
- 1 pound shrimp
- 1/2 tsp. dried red pepper flakes (to taste).
- 1/4 cup cilantro
- 1/2 cups fish broth
- 1/4 cup tomato paste.

Instructions

Put ingredients in the slow cooker. Cover, and cook on low for 8 hours.

Venison Green Beans Onion Stew

Serves 2

Ingredients - Allergies: SF, GF, DF, EF, NF

- 1 cup quartered onions
- 1 tbsp. coconut oil
- Salt, ground black pepper to taste
- 1 pound venison meat
- 1/4 tsp. dried red pepper flakes (to taste).
- 1 whole clove (discard after cooking)
- 1/2 cup beef broth
- 1/2 cup green beans

Instructions

Put ingredients in the slow cooker. Cover, and cook on low for 8 hours.

Pork Cauliflower Stew

Serves 2

Ingredients - Allergies: SF, GF, DF, EF, NF

- 1/2 cups chopped onions
- 1 tbsp. coconut oil
- Salt, ground black pepper to taste
- 1 pound pork neck meat
- 1/4 cup sliced green onions
- 1/4 cup chopped carrots
- 1/2 cups beef broth
- 3/4 cups cauliflower
- 1/2 cup sliced tomatoes

Instructions

Put ingredients in the slow cooker. Cover, and cook on low for 8 hours. Sprinkle with sliced green onions.

Sweet Potato Veal Stew

Serves 2

Ingredients - Allergies: SF, GF, DF, EF, NF

- 1/2 cups chopped onions
- 1 tbsp. coconut oil
- Salt, ground black pepper to taste
- 1 pound veal neck meat
- 3/4 cups chopped sweet potato
- 1/2 cups beef broth

Instructions

Put ingredients in the slow cooker. Cover, and cook on low for 8 hours.

Pork Broccoli Carrot Stew

Serves 2

Ingredients - Allergies: SF, GF, DF, EF, NF

- 1/2 cups chopped onions
- 1 tbsp. coconut oil
- Salt, ground black pepper to taste
- 1 pound cubed pork meat
- 1 cup broccoli
- 1/2 cups beef broth
- 1/2 cups sliced carrots

Instructions

Put ingredients in the slow cooker. Cover, and cook on low for 8 hours.

Moroccan Lamb & Mushrooms Stew

Serves 2

Ingredients - Allergies: SF, GF, DF, EF, NF

- 1/2 cups chopped onions
- 1 tbsp. coconut oil
- Salt, ground black pepper to taste
- 1 pound lamb neck meat
- 1/4 tsp. each: cumin, coriander, fennel seeds
- 1/4 tsp. dried red pepper flakes (to taste).
- 1/4 cup dried apricots
- 1/4 cup beef broth
- 1/4 cup tomato paste.
- 1/2 cups whole mushrooms
- ½ cup cilantro

Instructions

Put ingredients in the slow cooker. Cover, and cook on low for 8 hours. Sprinkle with cilantro.

Shrimp Peppers Stew

Serves 2

Ingredients - Allergies: SF, GF, DF, EF, NF

- 1/2 cups chopped onions
- 1 tbsp. coconut oil
- Salt, ground black pepper to taste
- 1 pound shrimp
- 1/4 tsp. dried red pepper flakes (to taste).
- 1 cup sliced red peppers
- 1/4 cup tomato paste.

Instructions

Put ingredients in the slow cooker. Cover, and cook on low for 8 hours.

Brown Rice Dishes

Paella

Ingredients - Allergies: SF, GF, DF, EF, NF

- 1/2 onion, finely chopped
- 2 tbsp. coconut oil
- 1 chopped garlic clove
- 1 chopped tomatoes
- Salt
- 1/2 tsp. sweet paprika
- A pinch of saffron
- 2 cleaned small squid, sliced
- 1 cup medium-grain brown rice
- 1 cups fish or chicken broth, plus more if needed
- 1/2 cup dry white wine
- 4-6 jumbo shrimps
- 4 mussels, scrubbed and debearded

Instructions

Put the oil in a paella pan and fry the onion until soft. Stir in the garlic and tomatoes. Add salt to taste, paprika, and saffron, stir well, and cook until the tomatoes get soft. Add the squid and the rice and stir well.

Bring the wine and broth to a boil in a saucepan. Pour over the rice, bring to a boil, and add salt. Spread the rice in the pan. Cook the rice over low heat for 20 minutes. Put the shrimp on top after 10 minutes. Once they become pin, turn them. When the rice is done, turn off the heat and cover the pan.

Steam the mussels and put them on top of the paella.

Asparagus Mint Lemon Risotto

Ingredients - Allergies: SF, GF, DF, EF, NF

For the risotto base
- 1 cup vegetable or chicken broth
- 1 tbsp. olive oil or avocado oil
- 1 small onion, peeled and finely chopped
- 1-2 sticks celery, trimmed and finely chopped
- 1 cup brown rice
- 1/2 cup dry white wine

For the risotto
- 1 bunch asparagus, woody ends removed and discarded
- 1 1/2 vegetable or chicken broth
- 2 Tbsp. coconut oil
- 1/4 bunch fresh mint, leaves picked and finely chopped
- zest and juice of 2 lemons
- sea salt
- ground black pepper
- extra virgin olive oil or avocado oil

Instructions

Chop asparagus discs, keeping the tips whole. Bring the broth to a simmer in a saucepan. Put the olive oil in a separate pan, add the celery and the onion and cook until soft. Add the rice and wine and turn up the heat and keep stirring.

Add the broth to the rice a ladle at a time, stir well and wait until it has been absorbed. When it's all absorbed, put to one side. Put a saucepan on high heat and pour in half the broth, followed by all risotto base and the asparagus. Simmer until almost all the broth has been absorbed. Add the rest of the broth in batches until the rice and asparagus are cooked. Turn off the heat, add olive oil, mint, lemon zest and all the juice. Check the amount of seasoning and add salt and pepper if needed.

Stir Fries

Pork and Bok Choy / Celery Stir Fry
Allergies: SF, GF, DF, EF, NF

10 oz. Lean Pork Tenderloin and 2 cups Bok Choy / Celery stir fry. Use as much veggies as you want or replace Bok Choy with Kale. Season with fish sauce.

Lemon Chicken Stir Fry

Ingredients - Allergies: SF, GF, DF, EF, NF

- 1/2 lemon
- 1/4 cup chicken broth
- 1 tbsp. fish sauce
- 1 teaspoons arrowroot flour
- 1/2 tbsp. coconut oil
- 1/2 pound boneless, skinless chicken breasts, trimmed and cut into 1-inch pieces
- 5 ounces mushrooms, halved or quartered
- 1 cup snow peas, stems and strings removed
- 1 bunch scallions, cut into 1-inch pieces, white and green parts divided
- 1 tbsp. chopped garlic

Instructions

Grate 1 tsp. lemon zest. Juice the lemon and mix 3 tbsp. of the juice with broth, fish sauce and arrowroot flour in a small bowl.

Heat oil in a skillet over high heat. Add chicken and cook, stirring occasionally, until just cooked through. Transfer to a plate. Add mushrooms to the pan and cook until the mushrooms are tender. Add snow peas, garlic, scallion whites and the lemon zest. Cook, stirring, around 30 seconds. Add the broth to the pan and cook, stirring, 2 to 3 minutes. Add scallion greens and the chicken and any accumulated juices and stir.

Pan seared Brussels sprouts

Serves 2

Ingredients - Allergies: SF, GF, DF, EF, NF

- 6 oz. cubed pork
- 2 tbsp. coconut oil
- 1 pound Brussels sprouts, halved
- 1/2 large onion, chopped
- Salt and ground black pepper

Instructions

Cook pork in a skillet over high heat. Remove to a plate and chop. In same pan with pork fat, add coconut oil over high heat. Add onions and Brussels sprouts and cook, stirring occasionally, until sprouts are golden brown. Season with salt and pepper, to taste, and put pork back into pan. Serve immediately.

Beef and Broccoli Stir Fry

Allergies: SF, GF, DF, EF, NF

- 10 oz. of lean Beef and 2 cups broccoli stir fry. Use as much broccoli as you want or replace Broccoli with Kale.

Garbanzo Stir Fry

Serves 2

Ingredients - Allergies: SF, GF, DF, EF, V, NF

- 2 tbsp. coconut oil
- 1 tbsp. oregano
- 1 tbsp. chopped basil
- 1 clove garlic, crushed
- ground black pepper to taste
- 2 cups cooked garbanzo beans

- 1 large zucchini, halved and sliced
- 1/2 cup sliced mushrooms
- 1 tbsp. chopped cilantro
- 1 tomato, chopped

Heat oil in a skillet over medium heat. Stir in oregano, basil, garlic and pepper. Add the garbanzo beans and zucchini, stirring well to coat with oil and herbs. Cook for 10 minutes, stirring occasionally. Stir in mushrooms and cilantro; cook 10 minutes, stirring occasionally. Place the chopped tomato on top of the mixture to steam. Cover and cook 5 minutes more.

Thai Basil Chicken

Ingredients - Allergies: SF, GF, DF, NF

Eggs
- 2 eggs
- 2 tbsp. of <u>coconut oil</u> for frying

Basil chicken
- 2 chicken breast (or any other cut of boneless chicken)
- 5 cloves of garlic
- 4 Thai chilies
- 1 tbsp. coconut oil for frying
- Fish sauce
- 1 handful of Thai holy basil leaves

Instructions

First, fry the eggs

Basil chicken

Cut the chicken into small pieces. Peel the garlic and chilies, and chop them fine. Add basil leaves.

Add about 1 tbsp. of oil to the pan.

When the oil is hot, add the chilies and garlic. Stir fry for half a minute.

Toss in your chicken and keep stir frying. Add fish sauce.

Add basil into the pan, fold it into the chicken, and turn off the heat.

Shrimp with Snow Peas

Ingredients - Allergies: SF, GF, DF, EF, NF

Marinade

- 1 teaspoon arrowroot flour
- 1 Tbsp. wine
- 1/4 tsp. salt

Stir Fry

- 1/2 pound shrimp. Peel the shrimp and take the vein out
- 1 Tbsp coconut oil
- 1/2 Tbsp minced ginger
- 1 garlic cloves, sliced thinly
- 1 cup snow peas, strings removed
- 1 teaspoons fish sauce
- 1/4 cup chicken broth
- 2 green onions, white and light green parts, sliced diagonally
- 1 teaspoons dark roasted sesame oil

Instructions

Mix all the ingredients for the marinade in a bowl and then add the shrimp. Mix to coat. Let it marinade 15 minutes while you prepare the peas, ginger, and garlic.

Add the coconut oil in the wok and let it get hot. Add the garlic and ginger and combine. Stir-fry for about 30 seconds.

Add the marinade to the wok, add the snow peas, fish sauce and chicken broth. Stir-fry until the shrimp turns pink. Add the green onions and stir-fry for one more minute. Turn off the heat and add the sesame oil. Toss once more and serve with steamed brown rice or soba gluten free noodles.

Pork and Green Beans Stir Fry

Allergies: SF, GF, DF, EF, NF

- 10 oz. of lean Pork
- 2 cups of Green Beans, snapped in half. Use as much veggies as you want or replace Green beans with Kale.
- 2 garlic clove, chopped
- 1 inch of peeled and chopped ginger
- Season with fish sauce.

Cashew chicken

Ingredients - Allergies: SF, GF, DF, EF, NF

- 1/2 bunch scallions
- 1/2 pound skinless boneless chicken thighs
- 1/4 tsp. salt
- 1/8 tsp. black pepper
- 2 tbsp. coconut oil
- 1/2 red bell pepper and 1 stalk of celery, chopped
- 2 garlic cloves, finely chopped
- 1 tbsp. finely chopped peeled fresh ginger
- 1/8 tsp. dried hot red-pepper flakes
- 1/4 cup chicken broth
- 1 tbsp. fish sauce
- 1 teaspoons arrowroot flour
- 1/4 cup salted roasted whole cashews

Instructions

Chop scallions and separate green and white parts. Pat chicken dry and cut into 3/4-inch pieces and season with salt and pepper. Heat a wok or a skillet over high heat. Add oil and then stir-fry chicken until cooked through, 3 to 4 minutes. Transfer to a plate. Add garlic, bell pepper, celery, ginger, red-pepper flakes, and scallion whites to wok and stir-fry until peppers are just tender, 4 to 5 minutes.

Mix together broth, fish sauce and arrowroot flour, then stir into vegetables in wok. Reduce heat and simmer, stirring occasionally, until thickened. Stir in cashews, scallion greens, and chicken along with any juices.

Meats

Baked Chicken Breast with Fresh Basil

Ingredients - Allergies: SF, GF, EF, NF

- 2 boneless skinless chicken breast
- 1/4 cup low-fat yogurt
- 1/4 cup chopped basil
- 1 tsp. arrowroot flour
- 2 Tbsp. oatmeal, coarsely ground

Instructions

Arrange chicken in a baking dish. Combine basil, yogurt and arrowroot flour; mix well and spread over chicken.

Mix oatmeal with salt and pepper to taste and sprinkle over chicken.

Bake chicken in 375 degrees in the oven for half an hour.

Roast Chicken with Rosemary

- 2 chicken pieces, skinned
- salt and pepper to taste
- 1 onion, quartered
- 2 Tbsp. chopped rosemary

Instructions - Allergies: SF, GF, DF, EF, NF

Heat the oven to 350F. Sprinkle meat with salt and pepper. Cover with the onion and rosemary. Place in a baking dish and bake in the preheated oven until chicken is cooked through.

Carne Asada
Allergies: SF, GF, DF, EF, NF

Marinade:

Mix together the garlic, jalapeno, cilantro, salt, and pepper to make a paste. Put the paste in a container. Add the oil, lime juice and orange juice. Shake it up to combine. Use as a marinade for beef or as a table condiment.

Instructions

Put the 1 pound flank steak in a baking dish and pour the marinade over it. Refrigerate up to 8 hours.
Take the steak out of the marinade and season it on both sides with salt and pepper. Grill (or broil) the steak for 7 to 10 minutes per side, turning once, until medium-rare. Put the steak on a cutting board and allow the juices to settle (5 minutes). Thinly slice the steak across the grain.

Meatballs

Baked Beef Meatballs

Allergies: SF, GF, NF

- 1/2 pound lean ground beef
- 1 tbsp. minced onion
- 1/4 tsp. minced garlic
- 1/2 tsp. parmesan cheese
- 1 egg
- 1/4 tsp. salt
- 1/8 tsp. pepper

Mix all of the ingredients in a large bowl using your fingers. Mix until the meat no long feels slimy from the eggs. Shape in small egg size meatballs. Place on a baking sheet. Bake at 375F for 20-25 minutes until the meatballs are cooked through. Serve with large Fiber Loaded salad with Italian Dressing.

Middle Eastern Meatballs

Allergies: SF, GF, DF, EF, NF

Ingredients

- 1 pound ground lamb or beef, or a mixture of the two
- 1/2 Onion, minced
- 1/4 of a bunch of fresh parsley or mint, finely chopped
- Ground cumin – 1/2 tbsp.
- Cinnamon -- 1 teaspoons
- Allspice (optional) – 1/2 tsp.
- Salt and pepper -- to season
- Coconut Oil – 2 Tbsp.

Instructions

Place the ground beef or lamb, onion, herbs, spices, salt and pepper in a bowl and knead well. Chill for 1-2 hours and let the flavors mingle. Form the meat into patties or balls the size of a small egg.

Bake in the oven on 350F. Serve with brown rice with tzatziki sauce.

Variations

Experiment with different seasonings--coriander, cayenne, sesame seeds.

Casseroles

Broccoli Chicken Casserole

Ingredients - Allergies: SF, GF, NF

- 2 cups broccoli florets
- 10 oz. skinless, boneless chicken (or turkey) pieces (breast or dark meat)
- 2 tsp of flax seeds meal
- Salt, pepper
- 2 eggs - beaten
- 1 cup of Yogurt Dressing (or coconut milk, if you don't like the sourish tang)
- 1/2 cup of chicken broth
- 4 tbsp. of grated low-fat cheddar cheese

Heat the oven to 400°. Cook broccoli around 5 minutes. Take broccoli out and add chicken (or turkey) and simmer for 15 minutes. Cut chicken (or turkey) into cubes and add it to the broccoli.

Combine broth, flax, salt and pepper in a pan and mix. Bring to a boil over high heat and cook 1 minute, stirring constantly. Remove from heat. Add yogurt dressing, beaten egg and then half of the cheese, stirring until well combined. Add sauce to broccoli mixture; and stir gently until combined.

Put mixture in a small casserole dish oiled with some coconut oil. Put remaining cheese on top, sprinkle. Bake at 400° for 50 minutes or until mixture bubbles at the edges and cheese begins to brown. Remove from oven and let cool for 5 minutes.

Beef Meatballs Broccoli Casserole

Ingredients - Allergies: SF, GF

- 2 cups broccoli florets
- 10 oz. beef meatballs (see separate recipe)
- 2 tsp of almond flour
- Salt, pepper
- 2 eggs - beaten
- 1 cup of Yogurt Dressing
- 1/2 cup of chicken broth
- 2 tbsp. of grated low-fat cheddar cheese

Instructions

Heat oven to 400F. Cook broccoli around 5 minutes. Prepare beef meatballs as in the recipe above. Combine broth, flour, salt and pepper in a saucepan, stirring with a whisk until smooth. Bring to a boil over medium-high heat; cook 1 minute, stirring constantly. Remove from heat. Add yogurt dressing, beaten egg and then half of the cheese, stirring until well combined. Add sauce to broccoli mixture; and stir gently until combined.

Put mixture in a small casserole dish oiled with some coconut oil. Sprinkle with remaining cheese. Bake at 400° for 50 minutes or until mixture bubbles at the edges and cheese begins to brown. Remove from oven and let cool for 5 minutes. Serve with large Fiber Loaded Salad with Italian Dressing.

Beef Meatballs Cauliflower Casserole

Ingredients - Allergies: SF, GF

- 2 cups cauliflower florets
- 10 oz. beef meatballs (see separate recipe)
- 2 tsp of almond flour
- Salt, pepper
- 2 eggs - beaten
- 1 cup of Yogurt Dressing
- 1/2 cup of chicken broth
- 2 tbsp of grated low-fat cheddar cheese

Instructions

Heat oven to 400°.

Cook cauliflower around 5 minutes. Prepare beef meatballs as in the recipe above. Combine soup, flour, salt and pepper in a saucepan, stirring with a whisk until smooth. Bring to a boil over medium-high heat; cook 1 minute, stirring constantly. Remove from heat. Add yogurt dressing, beaten egg and then half of the cheese, stirring until well combined. Add sauce to cauliflower mixture; and stir gently until combined.

Put mixture in a small casserole dish oiled with some coconut oil. Sprinkle with remaining cheese. Bake at 400° for 50 minutes or until mixture bubbles at the edges and cheese begins to brown. Remove from oven and let cool for 5 minutes. Serve with large Fiber Loaded Salad with Italian Dressing.

Cabbage Roll Casserole

Ingredients - Allergies: SF, GF, DF, EF, NF

1/2 pounds ground beef
1/4 cup chopped onion
1 cup tomato sauce
1 pound cabbage or sauerkraut leaves
1/4 cup uncooked brown rice
1/4 tsp. salt
1/2 cup beef broth

Instructions

Heat oven to 350F.
Brown beef in coconut oil in a skillet over medium high heat until through. In a large mixing bowl combine the onion, rice and salt. Add meat and mix all together. Roll mixture into cabbage leaves and arrange them in a casserole dish. Pour broth and tomato sauce over rolls and bake in the preheated oven, covered, for 1 hour.

Pork Chop Casserole

Ingredients - Allergies: SF, GF, DF, EF, NF

- 1/2 cup vegetable broth
- 1/4 cup brown rice
- 4 ounce mushrooms
- salt and pepper to taste
- 2 thick pork chops

Instructions

Heat oven to 350F. Pour broth into a baking dish. Add rice and mushrooms and mix. Salt and pepper to taste. Add pork chops in a single layer on that mixture and push them down into mixture and make sure they are covered with it.
Cover baking dish with aluminum foil and bake for 1 hour.

Mushrooms Casserole

Instructions – Allergies: SF, GF, NF

- 1 1/2 pounds sliced mushrooms (shiitake preferably)
- 1/2 pound sliced leeks
- Salt and freshly ground black pepper
- 1/2 tbsp. chopped parsley
- 1 beaten egg
- 1/2 cup of low-fat Greek yogurt
- 1/4 cup of shredded cheddar cheese, low-fat
- 1/2 pound cubed skinless boneless chicken (or turkey) breasts

Instructions

Heat oven to 375 degrees F. Mix beaten eggs and low-fat yogurt in a separate dish. In a casserole, place 1 layer of mushrooms, leeks and chicken cubes and season with salt, pepper, and parsley. Cover with 1/2 of a cup of eggs/yogurt mixture. Repeat process 2 more times and cover with shredded cheese. Bake until mushrooms and chicken is tender and crust is golden brown. Serve with Large Fiber Loaded salad with Italian Dressing.

Chicken Eggplant Casserole

Ingredients – Allergies: SF, GF, NF

- 1 pound Eggplant
- Salt and ground black pepper
- 1/2 tbsp. chopped parsley
- 1 beaten eggs
- 1/2 cup of low-fat Greek yogurt
- 1/4 cup of shredded cheddar cheese, low-fat
- 1/2 pound cubed skinless boneless chicken (or turkey) breasts

Instructions

Preheat oven to 375 degrees F. Mix beaten eggs and low-fat yogurt in a separate dish. In a casserole, place 1 layer of eggplant and meat cubes. Sprinkle with salt, pepper, and parsley. Cover with 1/2 of a cup of eggs/yogurt mixture. Repeat process 2 more times and cover with shredded cheese. Bake until eggplant and chicken are tender and crust is golden brown, about 20 minutes. Serve with Large Fiber Loaded salad with Italian Dressing.

Beef Meatballs Green Beans Casserole

Ingredients - Allergies: SF, GF

- 2 cups green beans florets
- 10 oz. beef meatballs (see separate recipe)
- 2 tsp of almond flour
- Salt, pepper
- 3 eggs - beaten

Half a cup of Yogurt Dressing

- 1/2 cup of chicken broth
- 4 tbsp. of grated low-fat cheddar cheese

Instructions

Heat oven to 400°.

Cook green beans around 5 minutes. Prepare beef meatballs as in the recipe above. Combine soup, flour, salt and pepper in a saucepan, stirring with a whisk until smooth. Bring to a boil over medium-high heat; cook 1 minute, stirring constantly. Remove from heat. Add yogurt dressing, beaten egg and then half of the cheese, stirring until well combined. Add sauce to green beans mixture; and stir gently until combined.

Put mixture in a small casserole dish oiled with some coconut oil. Sprinkle with remaining cheese. Bake at 400° for 50 minutes or until mixture bubbles at the edges and cheese begins to brown. Remove from oven and let cool for 5 minutes. Serve with large Fiber Loaded Salad with Italian Dressing.

"Breaded" "fried" food
Breaded Tilapia

Ingredients - Allergies: SF, GF, DF, NF

- 1/2 cup coconut meal for breading
- 1/4 tsp. pepper
- 1/4 tsp. minced garlic
- 1/4 tsp. paprika
- 1/8 tsp. salt
- 1 large egg whites (or whole eggs), beaten
- 1/2 pound tilapia fillets, cut into 1/2-by-3-inch strips

Instructions

Heat oven to 400°F. Set a wire rack on a baking sheet and coat with some coconut oil.

Place coconut, pepper, garlic, paprika and salt in a blender and process until finely ground. Transfer to a shallow dish.

Place egg whites in a second dish. Dip every piece of fish in the egg and then coat all sides with the coconut breading mixture. Place on the prepared rack. Sprinkle some drops of olive oil over each piece.

Bake until the fish is cooked through. Breading should be golden brown. Serve with large Fiber loaded salad.

Breaded Chicken

Ingredients - Allergies: SF, GF, DF, NF

- 1/2 cup flax seeds meal for breading
- 1/4 tsp. pepper
- 1/4 tsp. minced garlic
- 1/4 tsp. paprika
- 1/8 tsp. salt
- 1 large egg whites (or whole eggs), beaten
- 1/2 pound skinless, boneless chicken pieces

Instructions

Heat oven to 400°F. Set a wire rack on a baking sheet; coat with some coconut oil.

Place flax, pepper, garlic, paprika and salt in a food processor or blender and process until finely ground. Transfer to a shallow dish.

Place egg whites in a second dish. Dip every piece of chicken in the egg and then coat all sides with the flax breading mixture. Place on the prepared rack. Sprinkle some drops of olive oil over each piece.

Bake until the chicken is cooked through and the breading is golden brown and crisp, about 8 minutes each side. Serve with large Fiber loaded salad.

Lemon Pork with Asparagus

Ingredients - Allergies: SF, GF, DF, EF, NF

- 1/2 lb. pork chops
- 2 Tbsp. buckwheat flour
- 1/4 tsp. salt
- 1 tbsp. coconut oil
- Pepper
- 1/2 cup chopped asparagus
- 1 lemons, sliced

Instructions

Place the flour and salt in a dish and gently toss each chop in the dish to coat. Melt the coconut oil in a large skillet over medium high heat. Add the chicken and sauté until golden brown on each side. Sprinkle each side with the pepper directly in the pan.

When the chops are cooked through, transfer them to a plate. Add the lemon slices and asparagus to the pan. When the asparagus and the lemons are done, add the chops back to the pan.

Pizza

Meat Pizza

Ingredients - Allergies: SF, GF, EF, NF

- 1/2 cup cooked and minced chicken breast
- 1/2 cup low-fat cheddar, shredded
- 1/2 tbsp. minced onion & few basil leaves
- 1/2 tsp garlic minced

Instructions

Preheat oven to 425 degrees Fahrenheit. Process chicken, onion and garlic together. Mixture will be a dense crumb consistency. Press chicken mixture on parchment paper on a cookie sheet. Bake for 12 minutes. Let cool for five minutes.

Top with 1/4 cup of tomato sauce, a handful of low-fat cheese, basil and mushrooms (shiitake). Bake for 6-8 minutes more, or until toppings are melted. Let cool for five minutes. Slice and serve. Alternatively, you may want to try cauliflower crust version:

Grate half of the large cauliflower and steam it for 15 minutes. Squeeze the excess water out and let cool. Mix in 2 eggs, one cup low-fat mozzarella, and salt and pepper. Pat into a 10-inch round on the prepared cookie sheet. Brush with oil and bake until golden. Add the topping as above.

Side dishes

Green Superfoods Rice

Ingredients - Allergies: SF, GF, DF, EF, V, NF

- 1/4 cup spinach or any other leafy greens
- 1/4 cup leeks
- 1/8 cup or more cilantro leaves or parsley
- 1/4 jalapeno or serrano pepper
- 1 cloves garlic
- 2 Tbsp. coconut oil
- 1/4 cup brown rice
- 1/4 cup quinoa
- 1 tbsp. flax seeds meal
- 1 cups water
- 1/8 tsp. salt (more to taste)

Instructions

Pulse the spinach, leeks, cilantro, pepper, and garlic in a food processor. Do it until they become very finely chopped.

Heat the oil in a pot over high heat. Add the rice and quinoa and stir continuously for 5-8 minutes, until the rice is starting to turn light golden brown. Add the water, salt. Cover and boil for 5 minutes. Stir, and lower the heat to simmer for another 10 minutes. Stir in the green paste from the step 1 and cook until the rice is fluffy. Serve with additional salt, cilantro leaves, and lime if desired.

Roasted curried cauliflower

Ingredients - Allergies: SF, GF, DF, EF, NF

- 2 cups cauliflower florets
- 1/2 chopped small onion
- 1/4 tsp. coriander seeds
- 1/4 tsp. cumin seeds
- 2 Tbsp. cup <u>olive</u> oil or <u>cumin</u> oil
- 1/4 cup lemon juice
- 1 teaspoons curry paste
- 1/4 tbsp. hot paprika
- 1/4 teaspoons salt
- 2 tbsp. cup chopped cilantro

Instructions

Heat oven to 450°F. Place cauliflower florets in large roasting pan. Add onions to cauliflower. Dry toast coriander and cumin seeds in a skillet over medium heat until slightly browned, about 5 minutes. Crush in mortar with pestle. Place seeds in bowl. Whisk in oil, lemon juice, curry paste, paprika, and salt. Pour dressing over vegetables and toss to coat. Spread vegetables in single layer and sprinkle with pepper.

Roast vegetables until tender, stirring occasionally, about 35 minutes.

Sprinkle cilantro and serve warm.

Roasted cauliflower with Tahini sauce

Ingredients - Allergies: SF, GF, DF, EF, V, NF

- 2 Tbsp. cup extra-virgin olive oil or avocado oil
- 1 tsp. ground cumin
- 1 smaller cauliflower head, cored and cut into 1 1/2" florets
- Salt and ground black pepper
- 1/4 cup tahini
- 1 cloves garlic, smashed and minced into a paste
- Juice of 1/4 lemon

Instructions

Roast cauliflower like in the previous recipe.
Meanwhile, combine tahini, lemon juice, garlic, and 1/4 cup water in a bowl and season with salt. Serve cauliflower hot or at room temperature with tahini sauce.

Baked Sweet Potatoes

Serves 2

Ingredients - Allergies: SF, GF, DF, EF, V, NF

- 2 medium sweet potatoes

Instructions

Heat oven to 425 degrees F. Quarter sweet potatoes and place them in a casserole with a lid. Bake until tender when pierced with a fork (40 minutes approx.).

Asparagus with mushrooms and hazelnuts

Ingredients - Allergies: SF, GF, DF, EF, V

- 1 tbsp. lemon juice
- 1/8 tsp sea salt
- Ground black pepper, to taste
- 1/2 pound fresh asparagus, ends trimmed
- 1 tbsp. coconut oil
- 2 cups mushrooms
- 1/4 cup green onions, sliced
- 1 tbsp. hazelnuts, toasted and finely chopped

Instructions

Add the lemon juice, 1/2 tbsp. of the oil, salt, and pepper in a small bowl. Boil water in a pan and add the asparagus. Boil for few minutes. Heat the remaining 1/2 tbsp. oil in a pan on high heat. Add mushrooms and cook them until they are soft. Add green onions and sauté 1 more minute. Add the asparagus, and cook another 3 minutes. Remove from the heat and slowly add in the lemon juice mixture. Add the toasted hazelnuts over the top.

Chard and Cashew Sauté

Serves 2

Ingredients - Allergies: SF, GF, DF, EF, V, NF

- 1 bunch Swiss chard
- 1/2 cup cashews
- 1 tbsp. coconut oil
- Sea salt (optional)
- Ground black pepper

Instructions

Wash Swiss chard and remove tough stems. Heat a skillet over medium heat, and add oil when hot. Chop Swiss chard into thin strips. Add Swiss chard to the hot skillet, along with cashews. Sauté only 1 minute. Season with sea salt and ground black pepper to taste and serve warm.

Cauliflower rice side dish

Serves 2

Ingredients - Allergies: SF, GF, DF, EF, V, NF

- 1 head cauliflower
- 2 Tbs coconut oil
- Sea salt, garlic, ginger or ground black pepper (optional seasonings)

Instructions

Place the cauliflower into a food processor and pulse it until a grainy rice-like consistency. Season with sea salt and ground black pepper. Meanwhile, heat a large pan over medium heat. Add coconut oil when hot. Sauté cauliflower in a pan with oil and any additional seasonings if desired.

Crockpot

Slow Cooker Pepper Steak

Ingredients - Allergies: SF, GF, DF, EF, NF

- 1 pounds beef sirloin, cut into 2 inch strips
- 1/2 tbsp. minced garlic
- 1 tbsp. coconut oil
- 1/2 cup Beef Broth
- 1/2 tbsp. tapioca flour
- 1/4 cup chopped onion
- 1 cup carrots
- 1/2 cup chopped tomatoes
- 1/2 tsp. salt

Instructions

Sprinkle beef with minced garlic. Heat the coconut oil in a skillet and brown the seasoned beef sirloin strips. Transfer to a slow cooker.
Mix in tapioca flour in broth until dissolved. Pour broth into the slow cooker with meat. Add carrots, onion, chopped tomatoes and salt. Cover and cook on high for 3 to 4 hours, or on low for 6 to 8 hours.

Pork Tenderloin with peppers and onions

Ingredients - Allergies: SF, GF, DF, EF, NF

- 1 tbsp. coconut oil
- 3/4 pound pork loin
- 1/2 tbsp. caraway seeds
- 1/4 tsp sea salt
- 1/8 tsp ground black pepper
- 1/2 red onion, thinly sliced
- 1 red bell peppers, sliced
- 2 cloves of garlic, minced
- 1/4 cup chicken broth

Instructions

Wash and chop vegetables. Slice pork loin, and season with black pepper, caraway seeds and sea salt. Heat a pan over medium heat. Add coconut oil when hot. Add pork loin and brown slightly. Add onions and mushrooms, and continue to sauté until onions are translucent. Add peppers, garlic and chicken broth. Simmer until vegetables are tender and pork is fully cooked.

Beef Bourguinon

Ingredients - Allergies: SF, GF, DF, EF

- 3/4 or 1 pounds cubed lean beef
- 1/4 cup red wine
- 2 Tbsp. coconut oil
- 1/4 tsp. thyme
- 1/4 tsp. black pepper
- 1 cloves garlic, crushed
- 1/2 onion, diced
- 1/3 pound mushrooms, sliced
- 2 Tbsp. cup almond flour

Instructions

Marinate beef in wine, oil, thyme and pepper for few hours at room temperature or 6-8 hours in the fridge. Cook garlic and onion in a pan until soft. Add mushrooms. Cook until they are browned. Drain beef liquid. Place beef in slow cooker. Sprinkle flour over the beef and stir to coat. Add mushroom mixture on top. Pour reserved marinade over all. Cook on low for 7-9 hrs.

Italian Chicken

Ingredients - Allergies: SF, GF, DF, EF

- 2 pieces of skinless chicken
- 2 Tbsp. almond flour
- 1/2 tsp. salt
- 1/8 tsp. pepper
- 1/4 cup chicken broth
- 1/2 cup sliced mushrooms
- 1/4 tsp. paprika
- 1/2 zucchini, sliced into medium pieces
- ground black pepper
- parsley to garnish

Instructions

Season chicken with 1 tsp. salt. Combine flour, pepper, remaining salt, and paprika. Coat chicken pieces with this mixture. Place zucchini first in a crockpot. Pour broth over zucchini. Arrange chicken on top. Cover and cook on low for 6 to 8 hours or until tender. Turn control to high, add mushrooms, cover, and cook on high for additional 10-15 minutes. Garnish with parsley and ground black pepper.

Slow Cook Jambalaya

Ingredients - Allergies: SF, GF, DF, EF, NF

- 1/2 Bell pepper, chopped
- 1/2 Onion, chopped
- 1 Medium tomato, chopped
- 1/2 cup Chopped celery
- 1 Clove garlic, crushed
- 1 tbsp. minced parsley
- 1 tbsp. Chopped thyme leaves
- 1 tbsp. chopped Oregano leaves
- 1/8 tsp. Cayenne & 1/4 tsp. Salt
- 4 ounces pork, chopped
- 4 ounces Chicken breast, chopped
- 1 cups Beef broth
- 1/4 pound Cooked shelled shrimp
- 1/2 cup Cooked brown rice

Instructions

Shell shrimp and halve lengthwise. Combine all ingredients except shrimp & rice in a slow cooker. Cover & cook on low 9-10 hours. Turn slow cooker on high, add cooked shrimp & cooked rice. Cover; cook on high 20-30 minutes.

Ropa Vieja

Ingredients - Allergies: SF, GF, DF, EF, NF

- 1 tbsp. coconut oil
- 3/4 or 1 pound beef flank steak
- 1/2 cup beef broth
- 1/2 cup tomato sauce
- 1 small onion, sliced
- 1/2 green bell pepper sliced into strips
- 1 cloves garlic, chopped
- 1/4 cup tomato paste
- 1/2 tsp. ground cumin
- 1/2 tsp. chopped cilantro
- 1/2 tbsp. olive oil or avocado oil & 1 tbsp. lemon juice

Instructions

Heat oil in a skillet over high heat. Brown the flank steak on each side (4 minutes per side). Move the beef to a slow cooker. Add in the beef broth and tomato sauce, then add the onion, bell pepper, garlic , tomato paste , cumin, cilantro, olive oil and lemon juice. Stir until blended. Cover, and cook on high for 4 hours, or on Low for up to 8 hours. When ready to serve, shred meat and serve with brown rice or quinoa and salad.

Lemon Roast Chicken

Ingredients - Allergies: SF, GF, DF, EF, NF

- 2 pieces skinless chicken
- 1 dash Salt
- 1 dash Pepper
- 1 tsp. Oregano
- 1 cloves minced garlic
- 1 tbsp. coconut oil
- 1/4 cup Water
- 1 tbsp. Lemon juice
- Rosemary

Instructions

Wash chicken and season with salt and pepper. Sprinkle half of oregano and garlic inside chicken cavity. Add coconut oil to a frying pan. Brown chicken on all sides and transfer to crock pot. Sprinkle with oregano and garlic. Add water to fry pan and stir to loosen brown bits. Pour into crock pot and cover. Cook on low 7 hours. Add lemon juice when cooking is done. Transfer chicken to cutting board and carve chicken. Skim fat. Pour juice into sauce bowl. Serve with rosemary and some juice over chicken.

Fall Lamb and Vegetable Stew

Ingredients - Allergies: SF, GF, DF, EF, NF

- 3/4 or 1 pound Lamb stew meat
- 1 chopped Tomatoes
- 1/2 Summer squash
- 1/2 Zucchini
- 1/2 cup Mushrooms, sliced
- 1/2 cup Bell peppers, chopped
- 1/2 cup Onions, chopped
- 1/2 teaspoons Salt
- 1 Garlic cloves, crushed
- 1/4 tsp. Thyme leaves
- 1 Bay leaves
- 1 cups chicken broth

Instructions

Cut squash and zucchini. Place vegetables and lamb in crockpot. Mix salt, garlic, thyme, and bay leaf into broth and pour over lamb and vegetables. Cover and cook on low for 7 hours. Serve over brown rice.

Slow cooker pork loin

Ingredients - Allergies: SF, GF, DF, EF, NF

- 3/4 pound of pork loin
- 1/2 cup tomato sauce
- 1 zucchinis, sliced
- 1/2 head cauliflower, separated into medium florets
- 1 Tbs dried basil
- 1/8 tsp ground black pepper
- 1/4 tsp sea salt (optional)

Instructions

    Add all of the ingredients to a crock pot.

    Cook on high for 3-4 hours or low 7-8 hours.

Sauerbraten

Ingredients - Allergies: SF, GF, DF, EF, NF

Marinade

- Water -- 1 cup
- Lemon juice – 1/4 cup
- Red wine – 1/2 cup
- Peppercorns – 1/2 tbsp.
- Juniper berries -- 4
- Whole cloves -- 2
- Bay leaves -- 1

Roast

- Beef rump or round -- 1 pound
- Salt and pepper -- to season
- coconut oil -- 1 tbsp.
- Onion, thinly sliced -- 1
- Carrot, cut into thin rounds -- 1
- Celery, thinly chopped -- 1 stalk

Instructions

Place the marinade ingredients (except lemon juice) into a pot and bring to a boil. Boil for 5 minutes then remove and cool to room temperature. Add lemon juice.

Place the beef in a large glass dish and pour the marinade. Make sure that beef is covered with the marinade.

Set the roast and its marinade in the fridge and marinade for at least few hours. Turn the beef once or twice daily.

Remove the roast from the marinade and season with salt and pepper. Brown the roast well on all sides and set aside.

Add the celery, onion and carrot to the pot and sauté until the onion is cooked translucent. Put the roast to the pot and add in the marinade. Bring to a boil, then reduce heat to medium-low. Cover the pot and simmer until the roast is fork tender.

Remove the roast and set it aside. Strain the sauce and discard the solids and return the liquid to the pot. Bring to a simmer and add in the salt and pepper and simmer for few minutes more.

Variations

- **Meats**: Pork, lamb or venison.
- **Marinade Variations**: Nutmeg, ginger, thyme and coriander.

Fish

Cioppino

Ingredients - Allergies: SF, GF, DF, EF, NF

- 1/4 cup coconut oil
- 1 onions, chopped
- 1 cloves garlic, minced
- 1/2 bunch fresh parsley, chopped
- 1/2 cup stewed tomatoes
- 1/2 cups chicken broth
- 1 bay leaves
- 1/2 tbsp. dried basil
- 1/4 tsp. dried thyme
- 1/4 tsp. dried oregano
- 1/2 cup water
- 1/2 cup white wine
- 1/2 pound peeled and deveined large shrimp
- 1/2 pound bay scallops
- 6 small clams
- 6 cleaned and debearded mussels
- 1/2 cups crabmeat
- 1/2 pounds cod fillets, cubed

Instructions

Over medium heat melt coconut oil in a large stockpot and add onions, parsley and garlic. Cook slowly, stirring occasionally until onions are soft. Add tomatoes to the pot. Add chicken broth, oregano, bay leaves, basil, thyme, water and wine. Mix well.

Cover and simmer 30 minutes.
Stir in the shrimp, scallops, clams, mussels and crabmeat. Stir in fish. Bring to boil. Lower heat, cover and simmer until clams open.

Flounder with Orange Coconut Oil

Ingredients - Allergies: SF, GF, DF, EF, NF

- 1 pound flounder
- 1 tbsp. white wine
- 1 tbsp. lemon juice
- 1 tbsp. coconut oil
- 1 tbsp. parsley
- 1/3 tsp. black pepper
- 1 tbsp. orange zest
- 1/4 tsp. salt
- 1/4 cup chopped scallions

Instructions

Preheat oven to 325F. Sprinkle fish with pepper and salt.
Place fish in the baking dish. Sprinkle orange zest on top of the fish. Melt remaining coconut oil and add the parsley and scallions to the coconut oil and pour over flounder. Then add in the white wine.
Place in oven and bake for 15 minutes. Serve fish with extra juice on a side.

Grilled Salmon

Ingredients - Allergies: SF, GF, DF, EF, NF

- 2 salmon filets
- 2 Tbsp. coconut oil
- 1 tbsp. fish sauce
- 1 tbsp. lemon juice
- 1 tbsp. thinly sliced green onion
- 1 clove garlic, minced & 1/4 tsp. ground ginger
- 1/4 tsp. crushed red pepper flakes
- 1/4 tsp. sesame oil
- 1/8 tsp. salt

Instructions

Whisk together coconut oil, fish sauce, garlic, ginger, red chili flakes, lemon juice, green onions, sesame oil, and salt. Put fish in a glass dish, and pour marinade over. Cover and refrigerate for 4 hours.

Preheat grill. Place salmon on grill. Grill until fish becomes tender. Turn halfway during cooking.

Crab Cakes

Ingredients - Allergies: SF, GF, DF, NF

- 1 lbs. crabmeat
- 1 beaten eggs
- 1 cup <u>flax</u> seeds meal
- 1 tbsp. mustard
- 1 tbsp. grated horseradish
- 1/4 cup <u>coconut oil</u>
- 1/2 tsp. lemon rind
- 1 tbsp. lemon juice
- 1 tbsp. parsley
- 1/4 tsp. cayenne pepper
- 1 tsp. fish sauce

Instructions

In medium bowl combine all ingredients except oil. Shape in to smallish hamburgers. In fry pan heat oil and cook patties for 3-4 minutes on each side or until golden brown. Optionally, bake them in the oven.
Serve as appetizers or as main course with large fiber salad.

Sweets

Superfoods Dark Chocolate

Instructions - Allergies: SF, GF, DF, EF, V, NF

Mix 1/4 cup of coconut oil with 1/4 to 1/2 cup of cocoa powder (unsweetened, ideally organic and unprocessed) and some raw [honey](#) to taste. You really should experiment with cocoa and honey amount. Maybe start with equal amount of coconut oil, cocoa and honey, mix it and then increase amount of cocoa to your taste. Form balls or put in the ice cube tray. Put it in the fridge and 1 hour later you'll have great homemade Superfoods chocolate!

Fruits dipped in Superfoods chocolate

Ingredients - Allergies: SF, GF, DF, EF, V

- 2 apples or 2 bananas or a bowl of strawberries or any fruit that can be dipped in melted chocolate
- 1/2 cup of melted superfoods chocolate (see earlier recipe)
- 2 tbsp. chopped nuts (almond, walnut, Brazil nuts) or seeds (hemp, chia, sesame, flax meal)

Instructions

Cut apple in wedges or cut banana in quarters. Melt the chocolate and chop the nuts. Dip fruit in chocolate, sprinkle with nuts or seeds and lay on tray. Transfer the tray to the fridge so the chocolate can harden; serve. If you don't want chocolate, cover fruits with almond or sunflower butter and sprinkle with chia or hemp seeds and cut it into chunks and serve.

Superfoods No-Bake Cookies

Ingredients - Allergies: SF, GF, DF, EF, V

- 1/4 cup coconut milk
- 1/4 cup cocoa powder
- 1/4 cup coconut oil
- 1/4 cup raw honey
- 1 cups finely shredded coconut
- 1/2 cup large flake coconut
- 1 tsp of ground vanilla bean
- 1/4 cup chopped almonds or chia seeds (optional)
- 1/4 cup almond butter (optional)

Instructions

    Combine the coconut milk, coconut oil and cacao powder in a saucepan. Cook the mixture over medium heat, stirring until it comes to a boil and then boil for 1 minute. Remove the mixture from the heat and stir in the shredded coconut, large flake coconut, raw honey and the vanilla. Add additional ingredients if you want. Spoon the mixture to a parchment lined baking sheet to cool.

Raw Brownies

Ingredients - Allergies: SF, GF, DF, EF, V

- 1 cups walnuts
- 1/2 cup pitted dates
- 1/2 tsp. ground vanilla bean
- 1/4 cup unsweetened cocoa powder
- 1/4 cup almond butter

Instructions

Add walnuts and salt to a food processor or blender. Mix until finely ground.

Add the vanilla, dates, and cocoa powder to the blender. Mix well and optionally add a couple drops of water at a time to make the mixture stick together.

Transfer the mixture into a pan and top with almond butter.

Superfoods No Bake Balls / Cookies

Instructions - Allergies: SF, GF, DF, EF, V

Mix one tbsp. of each unsweetened coconut flakes, ground cashews, walnuts, almonds, goji berries, cacao, flax meal or chia seeds and one or two mashed bananas and spice it up with cinnamon and nutmeg. Make balls and freeze them. You can have 2 balls per snack if you crave sweets. You can flatten balls and have cookies instead.

Superfoods Ice cream

Allergies: SF, GF, DF, EF, V, NF

Freeze a banana cut into chunks and process it in blender once frozen and add half a tsp. of cinnamon or 1 tsp. of cocoa or both and eat it as ice-cream.

Other option would be to add one spoon of <u>almond</u> butter and mix it with mashed banana, it's also a delicious ice cream.

Apple Spice Cookies

Ingredients - Allergies: SF, GF, DF, EF, V

- 1/2 cup unsweetened almond butter
- 1/4 cup raw honey
- 1 egg & 1/2 tsp salt
- 1 apple, diced
- 1/2 tsp cinnamon
- a pinch of ground cloves
- 1/8 tsp nutmeg
- 1 tsp fresh ginger, grated

Instructions

Heat oven to 350 degrees F. Combine almond butter, egg, raw honey and salt in a bowl. Add apple, spices, and ginger and stir. Spoon batter onto a baking sheet 1 inches apart. Bake until set. Remove cookies and allow to cool on a cooling rack.

Superfoods Macaroons

Ingredients - Allergies: SF, GF, DF, NF

- 3 egg whites
- 1/2 cup coconut sugar
- 1/4 tsp. salt
- 1 cup unsweetened flaked coconut
- 1/2 cup soft dried apricots, coarsely chopped (3 ounces)

Heat the oven to 325 degrees. Whisk together egg whites, sugar, and salt in a bowl until frothy. Add apricots and coconut and mix to combine.

Shape mixture into mounds with hands and place one inch apart on baking sheet.

Bake until lightly golden, 35 to 40 minutes. Rotate sheet halfway through. You can cover them with Superfoods Dark Chocolate.

Superfoods Stuffed Apples

Allergies: SF, GF, DF, EF, V

Core 4 apples, fill them with Superfoods No Bake Balls mix and bake them in the oven for 25-30 minutes.

Whipped Coconut cream

Ingredients - Allergies: SF, GF, DF, EF, V, NF

- 2 cups of any fresh berries
- 1/2 lemons
- 1 can full fat coconut milk (14 oz.), refrigerated overnight
- 1 tsp of ground vanilla bean
- 2 Tbsp. raw honey
- Dash of cardamom, nutmeg and clove (optional)

Instructions

Separate coconut cream from the milk by putting it overnight in the fridge. Don't shake it before opening.

Open the can of coconut milk and scrape out the cream into a bowl. Use the saved milk for smoothies or other recipes.

Add cardamom, raw honey and vanilla. Whip the cream with a hand mixer until fluffy. Put in the fridge.

Wash berries and place in serving bowls or glasses. Squeeze the lemon over the berries. Place a big scoop of cream on top of the berries and serve.

Granola Mix

Ingredients - Allergies: SF, GF, DF, EF, V

- 2 Cup Rolled Oats
- 1/4 cup Shredded Coconut
- 1/2 Cup Raw Sunflower Seeds
- 1/4 Cup Sesame Seeds or Chia seeds
- 1/2 Cup Chopped Nuts
- 1/2 Cup -Water
- 1/2 Cup coconut oil
- 1/4 Cup raw honey
- 1/2 Tsp. Salt
- 1/2 Tsp. Cinnamon
- 1/4 tbsp. of ground vanilla bean
- Dried cranberries

Instructions

Turn the oven on and heat oven to 300F. Combine oats, coconut, sunflower seeds, sesame seed, cranberries and nuts (can include almonds, pecans, walnuts, or a combination of all of them). Blend well.
Combine water, oil, raw honey, salt, cinnamon and vanilla in a large pan. Heat until raw honey is dissolved, but don't boil.
Pour the honey over the dry ingredients and stir well. Spread onto cookie sheets. Bake 25 to 30 minutes, and stir occasionally. Let it cool. Store in a cool dry place.

"Peanut" Butter Truffles

Ingredients - Allergies: SF, GF, DF, EF, V

- 5 tbsp. sunflower seed butter
- 1 tbsp. coconut oil
- 1 tbsp. raw honey
- 1 teaspoons ground vanilla bean
- 3/4 cup almond flour
- 1 tbsp. flax seeds meal
- pinch of salt
- 1 tbsp. cacao butter
- Chopped almonds (optional)
- 1/4 cup Superfoods Chocolate

Instructions

Add sunflower seed butter, coconut oil, raw honey, vanilla, almond flour, flaxseed meal and salt to a large bowl.

Mix until all ingredients are incorporated.

Roll the dough into balls one-inch in diameter, place them on parchment paper and refrigerate for half an hour (yield about 14 truffles)

Dip each truffle in the melted Superfoods Chocolate, one at the time, and place them back on the pan with parchment paper or sprinkle with cocoa powder.

Pumpkin Brownies

Ingredients

- 1/3 cup almond flour
- 1/4 teaspoon baking powder
- 1/4 teaspoon salt
- 1/3 cup coconut oil, melted
- 1/2 cups raw honey
- 1 teaspoons ground vanilla bean
- 2 eggs
- 1/2 teaspoon of cocoa powder
- 1/2 cup pumpkin puree
- 1/4 cup chopped pecans
- 1/3 teaspoon ground cinnamon
- 1/4 teaspoon ground cloves
- 1/4 teaspoon ground nutmeg
- Sprinkle with crushed pumpkin and sunflower seeds and hemp hearts

Instructions

Preheat oven to 350 degrees F and grease a baking pan. Mix the almond flour, baking powder, and salt together in a bowl.

In another bowl, mix together the melted coconut oil, honey, and vanilla bean. Beat in the eggs one at a time. Slowly add the flour mixture and stir. Add cocoa powder, pumpkin puree, pecans, cinnamon, cloves, and nutmeg.

Spread the batter into the bottom of the baking pan. Bake until a toothpick inserted comes out clean, 45 to 50 minutes. Cool in the pan, cut and serve.

Vegan Sesame Seeds Cookies

Ingredients

1/2 cup toasted sesame seeds

1/3 cup almond flour

2 Tbsp. raw honey

1/8 teaspoon baking powder

2 Tbsp. coconut oil (or tahini)

1/8 cup water

1 Tbsp. lemon juice

1/8 teaspoon ground vanilla bean

Instructions

Heat oven to 350F degrees F. Blend all ingredients until you get a sticky ball. Make cookies and put them on baking tray. Bake for 20 minutes at 330F, until the cookies turn slightly brown. Take them out and cool.

Coconut Cream Tart

Crust

- 1 cups almonds, soaked overnight and drained
- 1/2 cup pitted dates, soaked overnight and drained
- 1/2 cup chopped dried apricots
- 1 tsp. ground vanilla bean
- 1 small banana

Filling

- 1/2 cup of flaked coconut
- 1/2 can of unsweetened coconut milk
- 1/3 cup of raw honey
- 2 egg yolks
- 1 Tablespoons of arrowroot powder
- 1 Tablespoons of coconut oil
- 1 teaspoons of ground vanilla bean
- 1/8 teaspoon of salt
- 1/4 cup of coconut cream

Instructions

Heat the ¼ cup of coconut milk, honey, salt and ground vanilla bean over medium heat in a medium size sauce pan. In a separate bowl, whisk the egg yolks and arrowroot powder. Add 1/4 cup of the warm coconut milk mixture to the egg yolks while whisking constantly. Then pour the egg mixture back into the coconut milk mixture and whisk until the mix thickens and then mix for 3 more minutes. Take off of the heat and mix in the coconut oil and flaked coconut. Cool and pour in the tart crust and refrigerate. Decorate with large coconut flakes.

Raw Vegan Reese's Cups

"Peanut" Butter Filling

- 1/4 cup sunflower seeds butter
- 1/4 cup almond butter
- 1 Tbsp. raw honey
- 1 Tbsp. melted coconut oil

Superfoods Chocolate Part:

- 1/4 cup cacao powder
- 1 Tbsp. raw honey
- 1/4 cup coconut oil (melted)

Instructions

Mix the "Peanut" butter filling ingredients. Put a spoonful of the mixture into each muffin cup.

Refrigerate. Mix Superfoods chocolate ingredients. Put a spoonful of the Superfoods chocolate mixture over the "peanut" butter mixture. Freeze!

HEALTHY EATING FOR TWO

Raw Vegan Coffee Cashew Cream Cake

Coffee Cashew Cream

- 1 cups raw cashews
- 1/2 tsp. of ground vanilla bean
- 2 tablespoons melted coconut oil
- 2 Tbsp. raw honey
- 1/4 cup very strong coffee or triple espresso shot

Crust

See recipe for Raw Walnuts Pie Crust

Instructions

Blend all ingredients for the cream, pour it onto the crust and refrigerate. Garnish with coffee beans.

Superfoods Reference Book

Unfortunately, I had to take out the whole Superfoods Reference Book out of all of my books because parts of that book are featured on my blog. I joined Kindle Direct Publishing Select program which allows me to have all my books free for 5 days every 3 months. Unfortunately, KDP Select program also means that all my books have to have unique content that is not available in any other online store or on the Internet (including my blog). I didn't want to remove parts of Superfoods Reference book that is already on my blog because I want that all people have free access to that information. I also wanted to be part of KDP Select program because that is an option to give my book for free to anyone. So, some sections of my Superfoods Reference Book can be found on my blog, under Superfoods menu on my blog. Complete Reference book is available for subscribers to my Superfoods Today Newsletter. Subscribers to my Newsletter will also get information whenever any of my books becomes free on Amazon. I will not offer any product pitches or anything similar to my subscribers, only Superfoods related information, recipes and weight loss and fitness tips. So, subscribe to my newsletter, download Superfoods Today Desserts free eBook which has complete Superfood Reference book included and have the opportunity to get all of my future books for free.

Your Free Gift

As a way of saying thanks for your purchase, I'm offering you my FREE eBook that is exclusive to my book and blog readers.

Superfoods Cookbook Book Two has over 70 Superfoods recipes and complements Superfoods Cookbook Book One and it contains Superfoods Salads, Superfoods Smoothies and Superfoods Deserts with ultra-healthy non-refined ingredients. All ingredients are 100% Superfoods.

It also contains Superfoods Reference book which is organized by Superfoods (more than 60 of them, with the list of their benefits), Superfoods spices, all vitamins, minerals and antioxidants. Superfoods Reference Book lists Superfoods that can help with 12 diseases and 9 types of cancer.

http://www.SuperfoodsToday.com/FREE

Other Books from this Author

Superfoods Today Diet is a Kindle Superfoods Diet book that gives you 4 week Superfoods Diet meal plan as well as 2 weeks maintenance meal plan and recipes for weight loss success. It is an extension of Detox book and it's written for people who want to switch to Superfoods lifestyle.

Superfoods Today Body Care is a Kindle book with over 50 Natural Recipes for beautiful skin and hair. It has body scrubs, facial masks and hair care recipes made with the best Superfoods like avocado honey, coconut, olive oil, oatmeal, yogurt, banana and Superfoods herbs like lavender, rosemary, mint, sage, hibiscus, rose.

Superfoods Today Cookbook is a Kindle book that contains over 160 Superfoods recipes created with 100% Superfoods ingredients. Most of the meals can be prepared in under 30 minutes and some are really quick ones that can be done in 10 minutes only. Each recipe combines Superfoods ingredients that deliver astonishing amounts of antioxidants, essential fatty acids (like omega-3), minerals, vitamins, and more.

Superfoods Today Smoothies is a Kindle Superfoods Smoothies book with over 70+ 100% Superfoods smoothies. Featured are Red, Purple, Green and Yellow Smoothies

Superfoods Today Salads is a Kindle book that contains over 60 Superfoods Salads recipes created with 100% Superfoods ingredients. Most of the salads can be prepared in 10 minutes and most are measured for two. Each recipe combines Superfoods ingredients that deliver astonishing amounts of antioxidants, essential fatty acids (like omega-3), minerals, vitamins, and more.

Superfoods Today Kettlebells is a Kindle Kettlebells beginner's book aimed at 30+ office workers who want to improve their health and build stronger body without fat.

Superfoods Today Red Smoothies is a Kindle Superfoods Smoothies book with more than 40 Red Smoothies.

Superfoods Today 14 Days Detox is a Kindle Superfoods Detox book that gives you 2 week Superfoods Detox meal plan and recipes for Detox success.

Superfoods Today Yellow Smoothies is a Kindle Superfoods Smoothies book with more than 40 Yellow Smoothies.

Superfoods Today Green Smoothies is a Kindle Superfoods Smoothies book with more than 35 Green Smoothies.

Superfoods Today Purple Smoothies is a Kindle Superfoods Smoothies book with more than 40 Purple Smoothies.

Superfoods Cooking For Two is a Kindle book that contains over 150 Superfoods recipes for two created with 100% Superfoods ingredients.

Nighttime Eater is a Kindle book that deals with Nighttime Eating Syndrome (NES). Don Orwell is a life-long Nighttime Eater that has lost his weight with Superfoods and engineered a solution around Nighttime Eating problem. Don still eats at night☺. Don't fight your nature, you can continue to eat at night, be binge free and maintain low weight.

Superfoods Today Smart Carbs 20 Days Detox is a Kindle Superfoods book that will teach you how to detox your body and start losing weight with Smart Carbs. The book has over 470+ pages with over 160+ 100% Superfoods recipes.

Superfoods Today Vegetarian Salads is a Kindle book that contains over 40 Superfoods Vegetarian Salads recipes created with 100% Superfoods ingredients. Most of the salads can be prepared in 10 minutes and most are measured for two.

Superfoods Today Vegan Salads is a Kindle book that contains over 30 Superfoods Vegan Salads recipes created with 100% Superfoods ingredients. Most of the salads can be prepared in 10 minutes and most are measured for two.

Superfoods Today Soups & Stews is a Kindle book that contains over 70 Superfoods Soups and Stews recipes created with 100% Superfoods ingredients.

Superfoods Desserts is a Kindle Superfoods Desserts book with more than 60 Superfoods Recipes.

Smoothies for Diabetics is a Kindle book that contains over 70 Superfoods Smoothies adjusted for diabetics.

50 Shades of Superfoods for Two is a Kindle book that contains over 150 Superfoods recipes for two created with 100% Superfoods ingredients.

50 Shades of Smoothies is a Kindle book that contains over 70 Superfoods Smoothies.

50 Shades of Superfoods Salads is a Kindle book that contains over 60 Superfoods Salads recipes created with 100% Superfoods ingredients. Most of the salads can be prepared in 10 minutes and most are measured for two. Each recipe combines Superfoods ingredients that deliver astonishing amounts of antioxidants, essential fatty acids (like omega-3), minerals, vitamins, and more.

Superfoods Vegan Desserts is a Kindle Vegan Dessert book with 100% Vegan Superfoods Recipes.

Desserts for Two is a Kindle Superfoods Desserts book with more than 40 Superfoods Desserts Recipes for two.

Superfoods Paleo Cookbook is a Kindle Paleo book with more than 150 100% Superfoods Paleo Recipes.

Superfoods Breakfasts is a Kindle Superfoods book with more than 40 100% Superfoods Breakfasts Recipes.

Superfoods Dump Dinners is a Kindle Superfoods book with Superfoods Dump Dinners Recipes.

Healthy Desserts is a Kindle Desserts book with more than 50 100% Superfoods Healthy Desserts Recipes.

Superfoods Salads in a Jar is a Kindle Salads in a Jar book with more than 35 100% Superfoods Salads Recipes.

Smoothies for Kids is a Kindle Smoothies book with more than 80 100% Superfoods Smoothies for Kids Recipes.

Vegan Cookbook for Beginners is a Kindle Vegan book with more than 75 100% Superfoods Vegan Recipes.

Vegetarian Cooking for Beginners is a Kindle Vegetarian book with more than 150 100% Superfoods Paleo Recipes.

Foods for Diabetics is a Kindle book with more than 170 100% Superfoods Diabetics Recipes.